GAME DAY
USC FOOTBALL

**The Greatest Games, Players, Coaches and Teams
in the Glorious Tradition of Trojan Football**

Library of Congress Control Number: 2006924577

This book is available in quantity at special discounts for your group or organization. For further information, contact:

Triumph Books
542 South Dearborn Street
Suite 750
Chicago, Illinois 60605
(312) 939-3330
Fax (312) 663-3557

CONTRIBUTING WRITER: Kevin Daniels

EDITOR: Rob Doster

PHOTO EDITOR: Tim Clark
PHOTO ASSISTANT: Danny Murphy

DESIGN: Anderson Thomas Design
PRODUCTION: Odds & Ends Multimedia

PHOTO CREDITS: Athlon Sports Archive, AP/Wide World Photos, Getty Images, Robert Beck/Sports Illustrated

Printed in U.S.A.

ISBN-13: 978-1-57243-882-8
ISBN-10: 1-57243-882-7

CONTENTS

Foreword

"We Are SC"

"Once a Trojan, Always a Trojan"

"Join the Trojan Family"

These are slogans that you hear...slogans that you see...slogans that you can even feel. Because these are slogans that have been, are and will be repeated for years to come, having been established by a proven winning spirit. Wherever there is a Trojan fan and a need for support, these slogans ring true.

I first became aware of the University of Southern California as a San Fernando High School football recruit. San Fernando High had just won the Los Angeles City Football Championship, and USC coaches came out to our campus to recruit me and others.

In 1969, as a high school recruit, I visited the campus of USC. And as an 18-year-old looking up at the Tommy Trojan statue on campus, touching the two Heisman Trophies and then meeting and talking with Mike Garrett and hearing him, as he looked into my eyes, tell me, "Once a Trojan, always a Trojan!" sealed the deal for me.

The significance of that decision still amazes me to this day. I have learned that the Trojan family extends literally around the world.

When young men and women are at that high school age, they all need to have their horizons broadened. Broadened to the extent that they understand, if they have family throughout the world, then they are and will be welcomed in those places. Whether for business, a social occasion or just recreation, they will be welcomed.

I visited Australia in 1977 as the first NFL player and Oakland Raider Super Bowl champion to play in the professional Rugby League for the Newtown Jets of Sydney. I was there between NFL seasons. While at the first game, a young boy came up to me and said, "My Dad went to USC." His father and family welcomed me and treated me warmly as part of the family, the USC Trojan family.

The Winning Tradition

The USC winning tradition has evolved as a result of its administration, coaches, players and fans.

The administration: USC's presidents, such as Rufus von KleinSmid, Norman Topping, John Hubbard, James Zumberge and currently Steven Sample, and athletic directors, such as Willis Hunter, Jess Hill, John McKay, Richard Perry, Mike McGee and now Mike Garrett.

The coaches: Gloomy Gus Henderson, Howard Jones, John McKay, John Robinson and now Pete Carroll, who has reignited the passions of the winning tradition often promoted by such key football figures as Nick Pappas and Marv Goux.

The players: Heisman winners Mike Garrett, O.J. Simpson, Charlie White, Marcus Allen, Carson Palmer, Matt Leinart and Reggie Bush. Also the historic legends, such as Brice Taylor, Cotton Warburton, John Wayne, Paul Salata, Frank Gifford and the McKeever twins, Mike and Marlin.

Many fans have heard of these and other great players on the radio or watched them on film, TV or videos. They saw when quarterback Craig Fertig threw that last-minute 15-yard touchdown pass to receiver Rod Sherman over the middle to upset Notre Dame in 1964.

I personally witnessed O.J. in the Rose Bowl cut across the field on a breakaway touchdown. How about Mike Garrett emerging from under a group of tacklers for a long, scoring punt return at California?

I saw quarterback Jimmy Jones connect with wide receiver Sam Dickerson in the back of the end zone for the game-winning touchdown against UCLA in 1969. I'm still trying to get credit from Sam "Bam" Cunningham for being the fullback each time he, as a tailback, dove up and over the stacked-up defensive linemen and linebackers into the end zone for those four touchdowns against Ohio State to win the 1973 Rose Bowl, helping us become the national champions for that season.

The impact of Sam Cunningham's contribution was not only legendary to USC but it was also an effective tool used by Paul "Bear" Bryant to break down the color barrier in the

South. Up until that point in time, African Americans had been blocked from attending major universities in the South. But Coach John McKay and Coach Paul Bryant were such good friends that, after USC beat Alabama in Birmingham in 1970 behind Cunningham's 135 rushing yards, Coach Bryant was allowed to present Sam to the assembled Crimson Tide players in their locker room as an example of what a "real football player" looked like.

Coach Bryant's deed points out a significant aspect of what life is about—human character. People are willing to sacrifice personal pride and risk their ability to sustain success in order that they, as a group, sustain their superior positions. Life is not a game, but there is a lot about games that can teach us a lot about life.

The USC Trojans' winning tradition, although disrupted for some short time periods, has remained intact and will continue for generations to come.

To have this book as a reference is a blessing! For how can you truly know and understand who you are and where you are destined to go unless you understand where you have been...your family history? All who have and will join the Trojan family will be inspired by the Spirit of Troy, and their lives will be blessed.

—Manfred Moore

Carson Palmer

Introduction

The images are unforgettable and too numerous to count.

The great tailbacks, from Mike Garrett to Marcus Allen, creating the legacy of Tailback U. The new millennium's Heisman parade through Los Angeles, starring Carson Palmer, Matt Leinart and Reggie Bush. Traveler, Tommy Trojan and the Song Girls. Unforgettable tilts with Notre Dame and UCLA. National championships won, legends created.

We're distilling the pageantry and drama of USC football into the pages that follow. It's a daunting task. Few college football programs in the country inspire the loyalty and passion that the Trojan football program exacts from its fans—and with good reason.

Through the words and images we present, you'll get a taste of what Trojan football is all about. Decades have passed since players first donned the cardinal and gold, but one thing hasn't changed: USC football is an unmatched tradition, a legacy of greatness, a way of life in Southern California.

TRADITIONS AND PAGEANTRY

The sights and sounds of game day at Southern California create an unmatched spectacle, a glorious mix of tradition and color and pomp and pageantry. Here's a small sample of what makes USC football unique.

—————— The Nickname ——————

Before 1912, USC's athletic teams were called the Wesleyans or the Methodists, names that didn't sit well with university officials. Then athletic director Warren Bovard, son of university president George Bovard, commissioned *Los Angeles Times* sports editor Owen Bird to determine a more fitting nickname.

According to Bird, "The athletes and coaches of the university were under terrific handicaps. They were facing teams that were bigger and better-equipped, yet they had splendid fighting spirit. The term *Trojan* as applied to USC means to me that no matter what the situation, what the odds or what the conditions, the competition must be carried on to the end and those who strive must give all they have and never be weary in doing so."

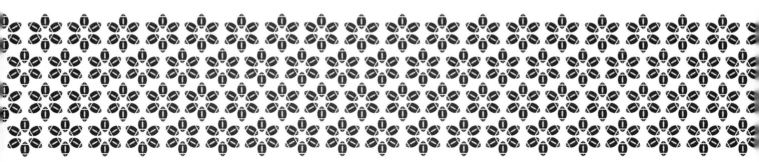

Cardinal and Gold

USC's school colors are a union of gold, the school's original color, and cardinal, the color of the College of Liberal Arts. In 1895, both were officially adopted as the colors of the university.

─── Spirit of Troy ───

The Trojan marching band, also known as the Spirit of Troy, is the most recognizable college marching band in the nation. It was established in 1880 and has played for seven presidents. The group has been featured in movies and television shows and earned a platinum album for its 1979 recording of "Tusk" with the rock group Fleetwood Mac.

The Spirit of Troy hasn't missed a Trojan football game, home or away, since 1987. The band numbers approximately 250 members, with 20 percent of them music majors and the rest from almost every school and department of the university.

Complementing the Trojan marching band are the USC Silks (tall flags), the Yell Leaders and the Song Girls, who were rated the No. 1 such group in the nation.

"Fight On"

Fight on for ol' SC

Our men fight on to victory

Our Alma Mater dear,

Looks up to you

Fight on and win

For ol' SC

Fight on to victory

Fight on!

Alma Mater
("All Hail")

All hail to Alma Mater,

To thy glory we sing;

All hail to Southern California

Loud let thy praises ring;

Where Western sky meets Western sea

Our college stands in majesty.

Sing our love to Alma Mater,

Hail, all hail to thee.

—— "Conquest" ——

The Spirit of Troy plays its famous processional march, "Conquest," after every USC score and victory. It was composed by Alfred Newman, musical director of Twentieth Century–Fox Studios, for the movie *Captain from Castile*. It was adopted by USC in 1954 for a basketball game against Oregon State and ever since has been emblematic of the championship tradition of the University of Southern California.

Song Girls

They are known worldwide as the USC Song Girls, and recently they were voted Best Cheerleaders in America by *Sports Illustrated*. The 2002 squad's captains were presented with the All-American Cheerleader Award. Officially known as the Song Leaders since the group's inception in 1967, they perform at rallies and alumni events as well as Trojan football and basketball games.

The Song Girls practice tirelessly to maintain the highest standard of any such group in existence. They work hand-in-hand with the Trojan Marching Band to coordinate their choreography with the halftime routines played by the band. All were trained dancers before entering USC—many have been dancing since childhood—and most were cheerleaders in high school. The pride they feel in representing the University of Southern California shines through in all of their performances.

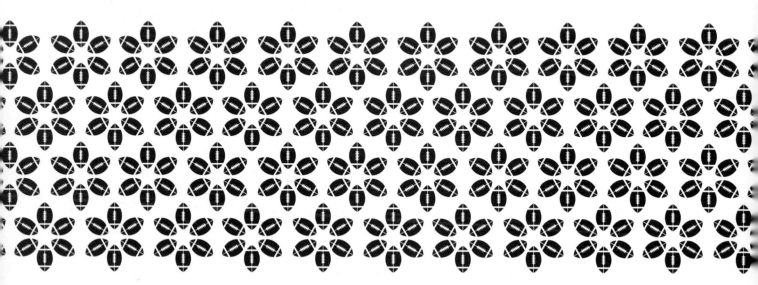

——— Yell Leaders ———

While the Song Girls are primarily a dance squad, cheerleading is primarily the duty of their male counterparts—the Yell Leaders. The group has been rousing Trojan spirit at rallies and athletic events for eight decades. The Yell Leaders are present at all men's and women's basketball and volleyball home games and are most remarkable for their physical stunts at football games. They travel with the team to South Bend, Indiana, for the clash with Notre Dame for the shillelagh and the Bay Area Weekender, when USC plays either Stanford or Cal. Being a USC Yell Leader requires year-round conditioning and a commitment taking second priority only to academics.

──── Los Angeles Memorial Coliseum ────

The Los Angeles Memorial Coliseum was built in 1923 and has been the home venue of the USC football team ever since. The Trojans beat Pomona College 23–7 on October 6, 1923, in the first football game ever played there. The Coliseum was the site of the 1932 Olympic Games and the track events of the 1984 Olympics. It has also been home to other football teams over the years, particularly the Los Angeles Rams and Raiders of the NFL. The Coliseum has a current seating capacity of 92,000.

Traveler

The white horse with the Trojan warrior astride is perhaps the most distinctive mascot in all of college sports. The horse's name is Traveler, and he made his first appearance at USC football games in 1961. Traveler VII currently reigns. The breed has been Arabian, Tennessee Walker or Andalusian, but he is always white. The first rider was Richard Saukko, who wore the costume worn by Charlton Heston in the classic film *Ben Hur*. The following year, 1962, he modified the costume to match the one seen on the Tommy Trojan on campus. Former USC defensive back and assistant coach Nate Shaw said of Traveler, "It definitely got the adrenaline going when I was playing, and I think it still has an effect on the players. When I was coaching against USC (at Oregon State), we hated to see that horse come down the tunnel because it got USC a little more pumped up."

Tommy Trojan

In the center of the University of Southern California campus stands the Tommy Trojan statue, unveiled in 1930 for the school's 50th jubilee. Sculpted by Roger Noble Burnham, the statue is a composite of many USC football players from the late 1920s, and particularly 1930 Rose Bowl Player of the Game Russ Saunders and All-American Erny Pinckert. At the base of the statue is inscribed "The Trojan" and the University's seal, and below the seal the words "Faithful, Scholarly, Skillful, Courageous and Ambitious," the qualities of the ideal Trojan. It stands as an emblem of the university's fighting spirit.

——— Shillelagh ———

The USC–Notre Dame series is the greatest and most storied intersectional rivalry in all of sports. Each year a trophy is awarded to the winner—a jeweled shillelagh. A shillelagh is a Gaelic war club made of either oak or blackthorn saplings, purportedly because they are the only ones tougher than an Irish skull. The foot-long shillelagh has ruby-adorned Trojan heads with the year and score of the SC wins, while emerald-studded shamrocks represent Notre Dame wins. According to legend, the original shillelagh was flown from Ireland by Howard Hughes's pilot and was first presented in 1952 by the Notre Dame Club of Los Angeles. The rivals are currently on their second shillelagh, the first one having been retired and placed on permanent display at Notre Dame.

Carson Palmer and the Trojans emphatically reclaimed the shillelagh after a 44-13 demolition of the Irish in 2002.

Victory Bell

America's greatest crosstown rivalry is the USC-UCLA football series, with the winner of each contest given yearly possession of the Victory Bell. Originally mounted atop a Southern Pacific Railroad locomotive, the UCLA Alumni Association presented the bell to the school as a gift in 1939. For two seasons, Bruin cheerleaders rang the bell after each UCLA score. After the opening game of UCLA's 1941 football season, six members of USC's Sigma Phi Epsilon fraternity drove away in the truck on which they had surreptitiously helped UCLA students load the bell. It was returned to UCLA at a ceremony on the USC campus in front of Tommy Trojan. It was decided in writing then and there that the 295-pound bell would be awarded annually to the winner of the contest.

Super Fan (Giles Pellerin)

Giles Pellerin was 91 years old when he passed away of a heart attack. Known as Super Fan, he had been to 797 consecutive USC football games, home and away, dating to the time of coaches Knute Rockne and Howard Jones. His streak began with the opening game of 1926 (the year of the first Notre Dame–USC game), his sophomore year as a USC student. The Trojans beat Whittier 74–0 that day. Since then he traveled 650,000 miles and spent more than $85,000 in pursuit of his passion— Trojan football. His passing came on November 21, 1998, at the Rose Bowl, while watching the USC-UCLA game.

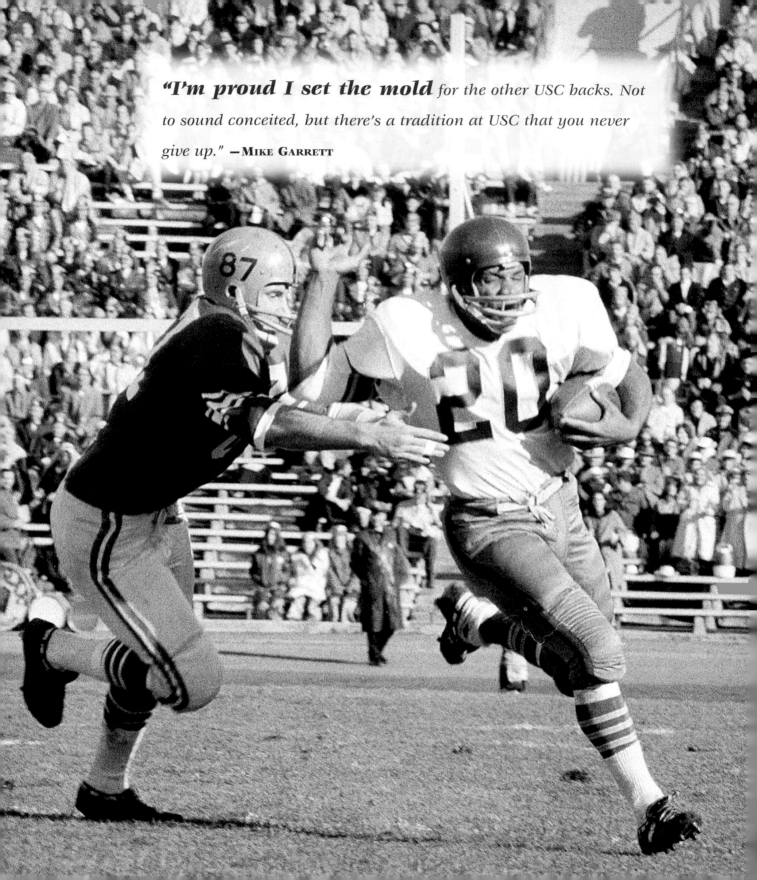

"I'm proud I set the mold for the other USC backs. Not to sound conceited, but there's a tradition at USC that you never give up." —MIKE GARRETT

THE GREATEST PLAYERS

USC's roster of greats reads like a who's who of college football legends. The names are familiar to fans of college football, and for the fans of the Trojans' rivals, they still bring a shiver of dread. Here are some of the stars who have shone brightest during their tenures in Los Angeles.

USC has had so many national award winners, so many great players, that they can't all be included here, which is why the following list should be considered representative, not definitive. We start with the Heisman Trophy winners.

The Heisman Parade

MIKE GARRETT

Tailback

1965 Heisman Trophy

Before embarking on a stellar professional career with the Kansas City Chiefs and San Diego Chargers, Mike Garrett was a two-time All-American at USC. He was the first of coach John McKay's great I formation tailbacks who inspired the school's nickname of Tailback U. He was also the first in a long line of Heisman Trophy winners to hail from USC—a group that

numbers seven now, tying Notre Dame for tops in that category.

Garrett set 14 school and conference records on his way to the 1965 Heisman. After compiling a then-unheard-of 1,440 rushing yards as a senior (1,000-yard rushers were almost nonexistent in those days), he set an NCAA record with 3,221 rushing yards over his three-year career, averaging 5.3 per carry and running for 25 touchdowns.

"The ball isn't very heavy. Besides, O.J. doesn't belong to any union, so we can work him as much as we want to." —COACH JOHN McKAY, IN RESPONSE TO THOSE WHO ASKED IF HE WAS OVERUSING SIMPSON

O.J. SIMPSON
Tailback
1968 Heisman Trophy

Mike Garrett set an NCAA career rushing record with 3,221 yards over three years. Simpson, USC's second Heisman Trophy winner, broke that record in two years. After transferring to SC from junior college, Simpson in 1967 and 1968 rushed for 3,423 yards, averaging 5.1 yards per carry and running for 36 touchdowns. He rushed for 1,880 yards and 23 scores in his Heisman year of 1968.

An unmatched combination of fluid grace and determination, Simpson was a unanimous All-American both of his years in the cardinal and gold. During his brief college career he set 19 school, Pac-8 and NCAA records.

Later he went on to break records in the NFL, where in 1973 with the Buffalo Bills he became the first back in league history to reach the 2,000-yard single-season plateau, with 2,003 yards.

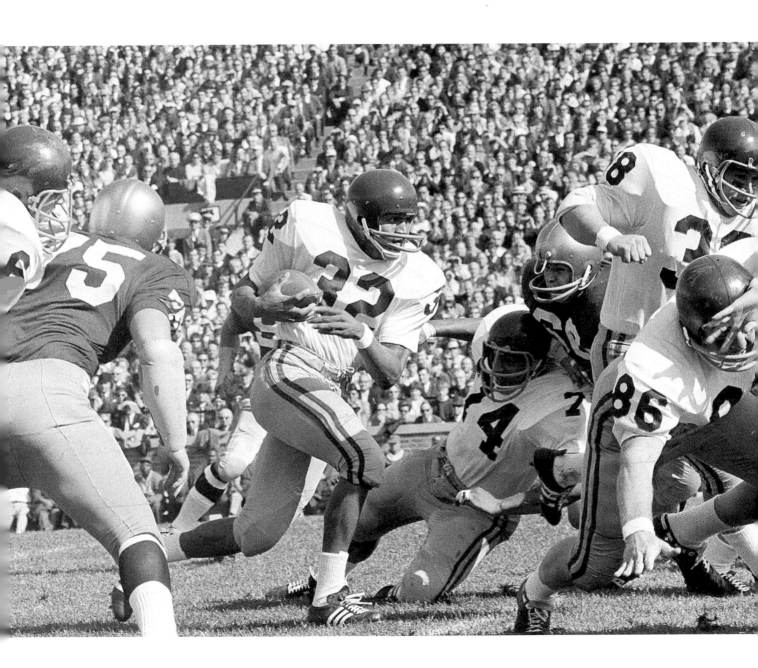

*The heart, guts and courage of Charles White were on display on Jan. 1, 1980.
White rushed for 247 yards and scored the winning touchdown (above) in USC's
17–16 Rose Bowl win over Ohio State.*

CHARLES WHITE
Tailback
1979 Heisman Trophy

White won the Heisman Trophy as a senior in 1979, when he led the nation in rushing with 1,803 yards, averaging 6.2 per carry. He ran for 19 TDs that year and for the second consecutive season led the nation in all-purpose running.

He finished his college career as the NCAA's second-leading rusher of all time with 5,598 regular-season yards. Postseason stats didn't count toward individual records in those days, but when bowl games are factored in, White ran for 6,245 yards for his spectacular career. Only four players have received two Rose Bowl MVP awards, and White is one of them. His numbers at SC also show 5.4 yards per carry and 49 rushing touchdowns, and he caught 59 passes over his four years as a Trojan.

White set 22 NCAA, conference and school records in all. He ran for more than 100 yards 31 times in his career, including 10 games during his phenomenal Heisman campaign.

"He's the best football player in America, a fierce competitor who is both elusive and powerful. He is the most durable football player I have ever coached. Other players occasionally get tired, but I think White could play a doubleheader." — WHITE'S COACH, JOHN ROBINSON

"I never considered Marcus a kid. He was like a grown-up playing with school kids."* —ALLEN'S HIGH SCHOOL COACH, VIC PLAYER

MARCUS ALLEN
Tailback
1981 Heisman Trophy

As former Trojan O.J. Simpson had done in the pros in 1973, Marcus Allen, USC's fourth Heisman Trophy winner, became the first college back ever to crack the 2,000-yard rushing mark for a single season. At the time, the achievement was hard to fathom, and it still represents one of the great campaigns in college football history.

His 2,342 rushing yards during his Heisman campaign of 1981 were a record then and still rank second all time behind only Oklahoma State's Barry Sanders's 2,628 in 1988. During his days in cardinal and gold, Allen broke 14 NCAA records and tied two others. He also set new NCAA marks with 212.9 rushing yards per game, 11 career 200-yard games and five consecutive 200-yard games.

Despite spending his freshman and sophomore seasons backing up 1979 Heisman winner Charles White, Allen finished his career with 4,682 rushing yards at 5.2 per carry, with 45 touchdown runs. And he also led the Trojans in receiving in both his years as a starter.

Allen spent 16 seasons in the NFL with the Raiders and the Chiefs, and he is a member of both the College and Pro Football Halls of Fame.

CARSON PALMER
Quarterback
2002 Heisman Trophy

When Carson Palmer won the Heisman Trophy in 2002, he became the first player not only from USC, but also from the West Coast, to bring home the honor in 21 years. Not since Marcus Allen in 1981 had a Trojan hoisted sports' most prestigious piece of individual hardware.

When it comes to Trojan Heisman winners, Palmer broke the mold. USC is called Tailback U because of the legacy left by former coaches John McKay and John Robinson, who coached a combined four Heisman-winning tailbacks at the school. But Palmer was a quarterback.

As a senior in 2002, his Heisman year, Palmer completed 63 percent of his passes for 3,942 yards and 33 touchdowns, all school records. He also set a new school standard by throwing for more than 300 yards in seven different contests that year. His 425 passing yards against Notre Dame in 2002 were the most ever against the Irish in a single game.

A four-year starter, Palmer finished his career as the Pac-10's all-time leader in both passing yards and total offense, setting or tying 33 school and conference records along the way.

"I couldn't be more honored to take this trophy back to share with my teammates in Los Angeles. This award is as much theirs as it is mine. A lot of people have been talking about the East Coast bias, and I think this takes care of that." —PALMER, FROM HIS HEISMAN TROPHY ACCEPTANCE SPEECH

"We've been on top for a couple of years now and have brought back the glory and tradition of the great USC football teams."

—MATT LEINART

MATT LEINART
Quarterback
2004 Heisman Trophy

For the second time in history, USC players claimed two Heisman Trophies in a three-year period—the first time, tailbacks Charles White and Marcus Allen brought home the hardware in 1979 and 1981, respectively. In 2002 and 2004 quarterbacks Carson Palmer and Matt Leinart had the honor.

Leinart won the Heisman as a junior, becoming the first Trojan to do so, when he completed 65 percent of his passes for 3,322 yards and 33 touchdowns with only six interceptions. Over his three-year career as a starter, he completed 65 percent of his tosses for 10,693 yards and a school-record 99 touchdowns and was an All-American all three years.

Perhaps more importantly, with Leinart calling signals, the Trojans were unmatched in the win column. USC went 37–2 with a 34-game winning streak, three Pac-10 titles and two national titles with Leinart under center.

REGGIE BUSH
Tailback
2005 Heisman Trophy

When Reggie Bush was announced as the winner of the Heisman Memorial Trophy in 2005, it marked the first time in history that one school provided three such honorees in a four-year period. With Bush at tailback, the Trojans lost only two games in three years—both by three points—and won two national championships.

The 200-pounder from San Diego's Helix High School possessed an utterly unique mix of skills and redefined the tailback position at Tailback U. He rushed for a career total of 3,169 yards, averaging 7.3 per carry with 25 rushing touchdowns. During his Heisman year of 2005, Bush averaged a phenomenal 8.7 yards per carry, netting 1,740 yards with 16 touchdown runs.

But he was also a major threat as a receiver. He was on the receiving end of 95 passes over his career with a 13.7-yard average per catch and 13 touchdown receptions. And he also shows four touchdowns returning punts and kicks on his career ledger.

"He's probably the fastest guy who's ever played at a running back position. Gale Sayers was very fast. O.J. was very fast. This kid [LaDainian] Tomlinson in San Diego is very fast. I think Reggie's faster than all of them. I believe that he'll get even better in the pros. Fundamentally, he'll get better. He's very special. Every time he touches the ball, you know he can go all the way. I think he's a fine back, and just as important, he's a good individual."* —USC AD AND FORMER HEISMAN TROPHY WINNER MIKE GARRETT

——— Trojans in the Hall of Fame ———

MARCUS ALLEN
Tailback, 1978–1981
Inducted 2000

O.J. SIMPSON
Tailback, 1967–1968
Inducted 1983

MIKE GARRETT
Tailback, 1963–1965
Inducted 1985

CHARLES WHITE
Tailback, 1976–1979
Inducted 1996

See "The Heisman Parade" on pages 23–35 for player bios.

JON ARNETT
Halfback, 1954–1956
Inducted 2001

Arnett was an All-American in 1955 and won the Voit Trophy as the Outstanding Player on the Pacific Coast in 1955 and 1956. He was first-team all-conference both those years. During his SC career, "Jaguar Jon," as he was known, led the Trojans in rushing, total offense, kick returns, punt returns and scoring. And in 1954, he intercepted three passes. Over his career he ran for 1,898 yards at 5.7 yards per carry and scored 30 touchdowns.

JOHNNY BAKER
Guard, 1929–1931
Inducted 1983

When USC won the national championship in 1931, Baker was a consensus All-American. He was first-team all-conference in 1930 and 1931. Besides playing guard, he also was coach Howard Jones's placekicker. Baker kicked the 33-yard game-winning field goal with a minute to play that gave the Trojans their first win over Notre Dame.

RICKY BELL
Tailback, 1973–1976
Inducted 2003

Bell was a unanimous All-American in both 1975 and 1976. Those two years combined he rushed for 3,390 yards and 27 touchdowns. In 1975 alone, he netted 1,957 rushing yards, a total that still stands third on the school's single-season rushing chart and is tops among all Pac-10 juniors of all time. For his career he averaged 5.2 yards per carry. In 1976 he was named conference Player of the Year.

Tragically, Bell died in 1984 at age 29. Atlanta Falcons general manager Rich McKay, whose father, John, coached Bell at USC, still has a picture of Bell on his office wall because "Ricky represents everything a professional athlete should be."

Ricky Bell

RAYMOND "TAY" BROWN
Tackle, 1930–1932
Inducted 1980

Brown was a regular on two USC national championship teams, in 1931 and 1932. As a senior in 1932 he was an All-American. He played in two Rose Bowls (1932 and 1933).

BRAD BUDDE
Guard, 1976–1979
Inducted 1998

Although the school became known as Tailback U, USC has an equally proud tradition on the offensive line, and Budde was one of the best. Budde was a starter all four years of his college career at USC, while the Trojans went 42–6–1, and was a three-time all-conference first-teamer, in 1977, 1978 and 1979. He helped the Trojans to the 1978 national title, and in 1979 he was a unanimous All-American, won the Lombardi Award and was the Outland Trophy runner-up.

Brad Budde

PAUL CLEARY

End, 1946–1947

Inducted 1989

Cleary played end for coach Jeff Cravath's Trojan teams. In 1947, Cleary made first-team all-conference and was a consensus All-American for the Pacific Coast Conference champions.

Anthony Davis (shown here skipping out of the arms of Oregon's Steve Donnelly) was one of the most electrifying players in college football history.

ANTHONY DAVIS
Tailback, 1972–1974
Inducted 2005

As a senior in 1974, Davis was a unanimous All-American. He ran for 3,724 yards and 44 touchdowns during his brilliant career. He sparked the Trojans to national titles in 1972 and 1974 and was the 1974 Heisman Trophy runner-up. He is best remembered for scoring 11 career touchdowns against Notre Dame, including six in 1972 and four in 1974. It was his second-half kickoff return for a touchdown that sparked one of the greatest scoring explosions in college football history, USC's 55–24 win over the Irish in 1974.

MORLEY DRURY
Quarterback, 1925–1927
Inducted 1954

Drury was a consensus All-American in 1927, when he became the first Trojan to surpass the 1,000-yard rushing mark in one season. He ran for 1,163 yards that fall, and this was in a day when 1,000-yard rushing seasons were almost unheard-of. No other USC back would run for 1,000 yards until Mike Garrett in 1965. Drury also was the first Trojan to run for 200 yards in a game.

JOHN FERRARO
Tackle, 1943–1947
Inducted 1974

A two-time All-American, Ferraro helped USC to three conference titles. He played in three Rose Bowls and was the school's first three-time all-conference first-teamer.

Frank Gifford's touchdown opened the scoring as USC ended top-ranked Cal's 38-game regular-season unbeaten streak with a 21–14 win in 1951.

FRANK GIFFORD
Halfback, 1949–1951
Inducted 1975

Gifford was an All-American in 1951, when he led the Trojans in rushing (841 yards), total offense (1,144 yards) and scoring (74 points). As a junior in 1950, he also notched a team-high three interceptions. He kicked a 22-yard field goal at Cal in 1949 that was the Trojans' first field goal since 1935. Gifford went on to have a brilliant career with the New York Giants and subsequently embarked on a distinguished broadcasting career.

MORT KAER
Halfback, 1924–1926
Inducted 1972

In 1926 Kaer became USC's first consensus All-American. He led the Trojans in rushing and scoring both his junior and senior years, and in 1925 he led the nation in scoring. He ran for 5.7 yards per carry with career totals of 1,588 yards and 36 rushing touchdowns. In the 1926 game at Cal, he posted USC's first ever 100-yard rushing game.

RONNIE LOTT
Safety, 1977–1980
Inducted 2002

Ronnie Lott was an All-Pac-10 first-teamer in 1979 and 1980 and was a unanimous All-American in 1980. He was a member of the Trojans' 1978 national championship team. He racked up 250 career tackles, including 22 for losses. He also registered 14 interceptions and 37 pass breakups. As a senior he picked off eight enemy aerials, tying for the NCAA lead, and deflected 16 other passes. Lott is undoubtedly one of the toughest, hardest-hitting players in the history of football.

MIKE MCKEEVER
Guard, 1958–1960
Inducted1987

McKeever was a three-year letterman (1958, 1959 and 1960) and an All-American in 1959.

An injury cut his college career short during his senior year of 1960. As a junior in 1959, he was first-team all-conference and captured USC's Davis-Teschke Award as the team's Most Inspirational Player.

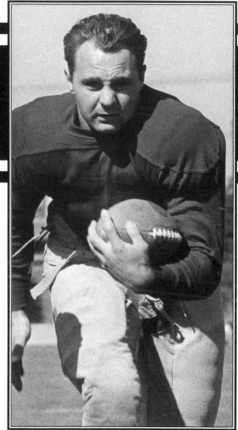

ERNY PINCKERT
Halfback, 1929–1931
Inducted 1957

Pinckert was a two-time All-American and all-conference first-teamer (1930 and 1931). He was a consensus All-American as a senior in 1931. He was a member of the 1931 national championship team and was MVP of the 1932 Rose Bowl, when he scored two touchdowns.

MARVIN POWELL
Offensive Tackle, 1974–1976
Inducted 1994

Powell was a three-time all-conference first-teamer (1974, 1975, and 1976) and a two-time All-American (1975 and 1976). He played for USC's 1974 national title team. He also played in the 1975 and 1977 Rose Bowls and was the fourth overall pick in the 1977 NFL Draft.

AARON ROSENBERG
Guard, 1931–1933
Inducted 1966

Rosenberg was a key player on two USC national championship teams, in 1931 and 1932. The Trojans were 30–2–1 during his career, went undefeated against Notre Dame (3–0) and put together a 25-game winning streak. He was a two-time All-American (1932 and 1933) and was a consensus choice as a senior in 1933. He also was a consensus all-conference choice as a junior and senior and played in two Rose Bowls (1932 and 1933).

ERNIE SMITH

Tackle, 1930–1932

Inducted 1970

Smith played for two national champions while at USC, in 1931 and 1932. The Trojans were 28–3 during his career and won two conference titles. He played in two Rose Bowls, in 1932 and 1933, and as a senior in 1932 he became USC's first unanimous All-American.

HARRY SMITH
Guard, 1937–1939
Inducted 1955

Smith was a two-time All-American (1938 and 1939). In his senior year of 1939, he was a consensus choice as the Trojans won the national championship. He played in the 1939 and 1940 Rose Bowls and also played rugby while at USC.

LYNN SWANN
Wide Receiver, 1971–1973
Inducted 1993

Swann is well remembered for his Super Bowl exploits as a Pittsburgh Steeler, but before that he was a college hero at USC. In 1972, the Trojans won the national championship as Swann caught 26 passes, averaging 21 yards per reception. As a senior in 1973, he caught 42 balls, including six for touchdowns, and he was a consensus All-American. Over his career at SC he caught 95 passes, averaging 16.4 yards per catch, and played in the 1973 and 1974 Rose Bowls.

COTTON WARBURTON

Quarterback, 1932–1934

Inducted 1975

Warburton was a member of USC's 1932 national championship team. At the conclusion of the year, in the 1933 Rose Bowl, he scored two touchdowns. The following season, he rushed for 885 yards at 5.9 per carry, scored 12 touchdowns and was a unanimous All-American.

RON YARY
Offensive Tackle, 1965–1967
Inducted 1987

In 1967, Yary became the first player from a West Coast school to win the Outland Trophy.

He was a consensus All-American in 1966 and a unanimous choice with the Trojans' national championship team in 1967. He played in the 1967 and 1968 Rose Bowls and was the No. 1 overall pick in the 1968 NFL Draft.

CHARLES YOUNG
Tight End, 1970–1972
Inducted 2004

Young was a unanimous All-American in 1972, when the Trojans won the national title. He broke onto the scene as a sophomore in 1970 by averaging 21 yards per catch from his tight end position. As a senior, he led the team in receiving with 29 catches. His career numbers show 68 receptions with a 16.1-yard average and 10 touchdowns. He was the sixth overall pick in the 1973 NFL Draft.

—————— Other Memorable Trojans ——————

GUS SHAVER
Quarterback, 1929–1931

Shaver was the quarterback of USC's 1931 national championship team. He led the Trojans in rushing that year with 936 yards and in scoring with 100 points. He tallied 16 touchdowns that fall and was a consensus All-American. He played in two Rose Bowls (1930 and 1932).

SAM CUNNINGHAM
Fullback, 1970–1972

In 1972, USC won a national title, and Cunningham was an All-American and team captain. He was the MVP of the 1973 Rose Bowl, when he scored on four short plunges into the line. He was known as Sam "Bam" Cunningham because of his battering-ram style at the goal line. He ran for 1,579 career yards and 23 touch-downs, including 13 as a senior. Legendary Alabama coach Bear Bryant used Cunningham's performance in USC's 42–21 win over the Tide in 1970 as the impetus to integrate the Alabama football team.

According to legend, Alabama coach Bear Bryant stood Sam Cunningham (shown above against Ohio State in the Rose Bowl) in front of his players and said, "This is what a football player looks like."

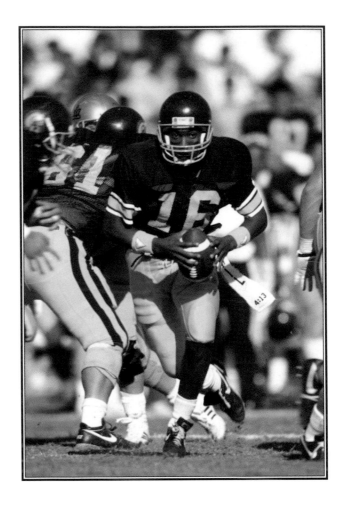

RODNEY PEETE
Quarterback, 1985–1988

As a senior in 1988, Peete quarterbacked Coach Larry Smith's Trojans to a 10–2 record. He won the 1988 Johnny Unitas Golden Arm Award, presented to the nation's top senior quarterback, and was the Heisman Trophy runner-up. He played in four bowl games, including the 1988 and 1989 Rose Bowls. Over his career, he threw for 8,225 yards and 54 touchdowns and ran for 12 more scores.

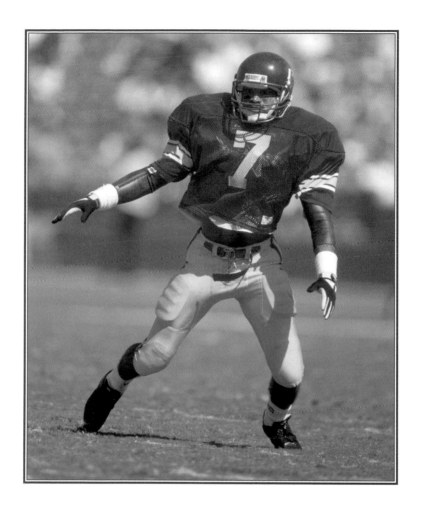

MARK CARRIER
Free Safety, 1987–1989

Carrier was a two-time first-team All-American, in 1988 and 1989. As a junior in 1989, he intercepted seven passes in addition to tallying 107 tackles, 10 pass deflections and three fumble recoveries. That fall he won the Jim Thorpe Award as the nation's best defensive back. He was a three-year starter with 13 career interceptions.

JUNIOR SEAU
Linebacker, 1988–1989

As a junior in 1989, Seau registered an incredible 27 tackles behind the line of scrimmage for losses totaling 148 yards. That year, he also deflected 12 passes and intercepted one, running it back 21 yards. Over his two years in cardinal and gold, Seau racked up 107 total tackles, including 33 for losses. He was a 1989 All-American and Pac-10 Defensive Player of the Year. He was the fifth overall pick as a junior in the 1990 NFL Draft.

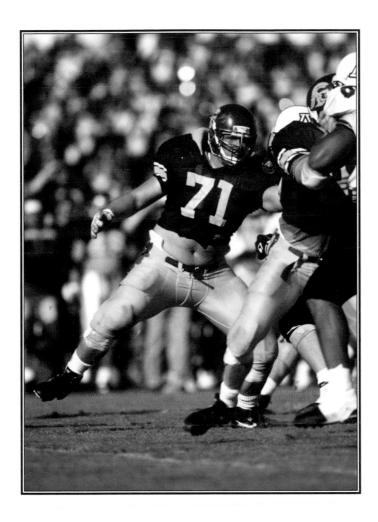

TONY BOSELLI
Offensive Tackle, 1991–1994

Boselli was a four-year starting offensive tackle at USC. He was a two-year All-American and was a consensus pick in 1994. He won USC's Offensive Player of the Year Award as a freshman in 1991. He was a three-time all-conference first-teamer and won the Pac-10's Morris Trophy as the conference's top offensive lineman as a senior. For years, he served as the prototypical NFL offensive tackle.

KEYSHAWN JOHNSON
Wide Receiver, 1994–1995

In just two years as a Trojan, Johnson caught 168 passes for 2,796 yards and 16 touchdowns. His senior year of 1995, he caught 102 passes and was a unanimous All-American. He was Offensive MVP of the 1995 Cotton Bowl, when he caught eight passes for game records of 222 yards and three touchdowns. He was 1996 Rose Bowl MVP when he caught 12 passes for a game record of 216 yards and a touchdown. He was the 1995 Pac-10 Offensive Player of the Year and finished seventh in Heisman voting.

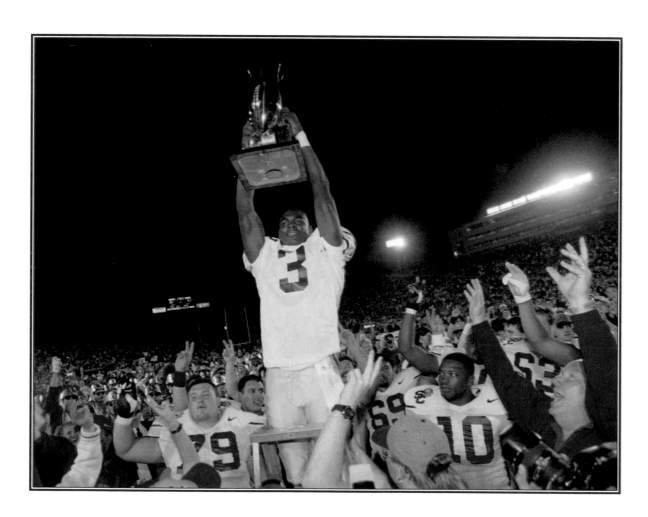

CHRIS CLAIBORNE
Linebacker, 1996–1998

As a junior in 1998, Claiborne led the Trojans in tackles (120), interceptions (six) and pass deflections (16) and won the Butkus Award, presented annually to the nation's best linebacker. He also was named the Pac-10 Defensive Player of the Year. He was a three-year starter who amassed 312 career tackles, 27 of them for losses.

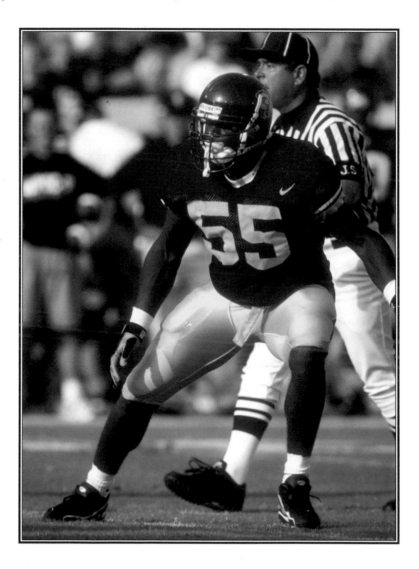

TROY POLAMALU
Safety, 1999–2002

Polamalu was a four-year letterman, a two-time All-American and team captain in both his junior and senior years. He was a 2002 Thorpe Award finalist. Over his career, he notched 281 total tackles, including 29 for losses, and deflected 13 passes. He also blocked four punts, including three in his junior year alone.

MIKE WILLIAMS
Wide Receiver, 2002–2003

In his all-too-brief career as a Trojan, Williams made a huge splash. He caught 81 passes in 2002 and 95 in 2003. He was a freshman All-American and Pac-10 Freshman of the Year in 2002. USC was 23–3 over his career, and he was a consensus All-American as a member of USC's 2003 national championship team. That season, he finished eighth in Heisman Trophy voting and was a finalist for the Biletnikoff Award.

THE COACHES

It has taken the leadership of great men to produce the legacy and tradition that embody USC football. Four Trojan coaches in particular stand among the greats the game has produced.

Howard Jones

The strongest language he ever used was "gol-dang," "ye gads" and "pshaw." His mind was so fixed on football he didn't see traffic signals and other cars as he drove, he lost his socks and keys, forgot appointments, often left members of his family stranded and sometimes forgot his way home. But Howard Jones was a ferocious competitor who carried on fierce rivalries with Knute Rockne and Pop Warner.

Before taking over as Southern California's football coach, Jones made coaching stops at Syracuse (1908); Yale, his alma mater, twice (1909 and 1913); Ohio State (1910); Iowa (1916–1923) and Duke (1924).

In his 16 years at USC (1925–1940), Jones coached seven Pacific Coast Conference champions, won all five Rose Bowls in which his Trojans participated and compiled a record of

JONES AT USC

YEAR	RECORD (CONFERENCE)	BOWL
1925	11–2 (3–2, T 3rd)	
1926	8–2 (5–1, 2nd)	
1927	8–1–1 (4–0–1, T 1st)	
1928*	9–0–1 (4–0–1, 1st)	
1929*	10–2 (6–1, 1st)	Rose
1930	8–2 (5–1, 2nd)	
1931**	10–1 (7–0, 1st)	Rose
1932**	10–0 (6–0, 1st)	Rose
1933	10–1–1 (4–1–1, 3rd)	
1934	4–6–1 (1–4–1, 7th)	
1935	5–7 (2–4, 8th)	
1936	4–2–3 (3–2–2, T 3rd)	
1937	4–4–2 (2–3–2, 7th)	
1938	9–2 (6–1, T 1st)	Rose
1939*	8–0–2 (5–0–2, 1st)	Rose
1940	3–4–2 (2–3–2, 7th)	

*national champions
**consensus national champions

The storied Southern California–Notre Dame rivalry began on Jones's watch, in 1926, and he once took three in a row from the Irish from 1931 to 1933.

Jones's Trojans took on coach Bob Neyland's Tennessee team in the Rose Bowl following the 1939 season. The Volunteers were unbeaten and finished the regular season without giving up a single point to the opposition. In fact, Tennessee had been unscored-upon for the last 15 games and 18 of the last 19, and was riding a 23-game winning streak. But SC gave Tennessee a dose of its own medicine on January 1, 1940, and prevailed 14–0.

121–36–13. Ten of his players were consensus All-Americans. He also won five national championships at USC, including repeats in 1928–1929 and 1931–1932. His 29-year career worksheet reads 194–64–21 (.733).

Jones was the brother of Tad Jones, another great Yale player and coach. Both the Jones brothers are enshrined in the College Football Hall of Fame, and Howard is a charter member (1951).

John McKay

John McKay was as charismatic and quotable as he was brilliant. "I'll never be hung in effigy," he once quipped. "Before every season I send my men out to buy up all the rope in Los Angeles."

In his 16 years as a college head coach—all at USC—McKay put together a record of 127–40–8, for a winning percentage of .749. During his tenure from 1960 to 1975, he won more football games than any other coach in school history.

McKay posted consecutive four-win seasons in his first two years while laying the groundwork for one of the most successful runs in history. In his third year, 1962, the Trojans finished 11–0, outscoring their oppo-

nents by 261–92, and were consensus national champions.

McKay seemed to win national titles every five years, like clockwork, as others followed in

Bob Hope presents USC coach John McKay (right) with the 1972 AP National Championship trophy as Jack Nicklaus looks on.

McKAY AT USC

YEAR	RECORD (CONFERENCE)	BOWL
1960	4–6 (3–1, 2nd)	
1961	4–5–1 (2–1–1, T 2nd)	
1962**	11–0 (4–0, 1st)	Rose
1963	7–3 (3–1, 2nd)	
1964	7–3 (3–1, T 1st)	
1965	7–2–1 (4–1, 2nd)	
1966	7–4 (4–1, 1st)	Rose
1967**	10–1 (6–1, 1st)	Rose
1968	9–1–1 (6–0, 1st)	Rose
1969	10–0–1 (6–0, 1st)	Rose
1970	6–4–1 (3–4, T 6th)	
1971	6–4–1 (3–2–1, 2nd)	
1972**	12–0 (7–0, 1st)	Rose
1973	9–2–1 (7–0, 1st)	Rose
1974*	10–1–1 (6–0–1, 1st)	Rose
1975	8–4 (3–4, 5th)	Liberty

*national champions

**consensus national champions

1967 and 1972. That 1972 contingent is without question McKay's masterpiece and one of the greatest football teams ever, anywhere. It averaged 39 points per game, outscored the opposition 467–134, skated through a rugged schedule without ever being seriously challenged and buried third-ranked Ohio State 42–17 in the Rose Bowl on the way to a 12–0 record. He finished his career 6–3 in postseason competition, including 5–3 in the Rose Bowl.

McKay's tailbacks are as legendary as he is. Among the great running backs who played for McKay were Mike Garrett, O.J. Simpson, Clarence Davis, Anthony Davis and Ricky Bell. Garrett and Simpson won Heisman Trophies in 1965 and 1968, respectively. It was under McKay, the inventor of the modern I formation, that USC became known as Tailback U. When asked by a reporter why his tailback carried the ball so many times, McKay replied, "Why not? It's not heavy." Vintage McKay.

John Robinson

As John McKay's successor, John Robinson had a tough act to follow. And he didn't disappoint. Robinson is one of only three head football coaches to post more than 100 wins at USC—he went 104–35–4 in two stints (1976–1982 and 1993–1997). His winning percentage at the Trojan helm is .741, up in the same lofty atmosphere as the other greats who went before him—Howard Jones and McKay.

Robinson played end at Oregon. After serving a stint in the army, he began his coaching career as an assistant at his alma mater. McKay then hired him to his staff, and he remained at USC for three years, then spent one year with the Oakland Raiders. The following year, USC hired him to succeed McKay.

Robinson got off to a rousing start in his inaugural season, going 11–1 and finishing with a No. 2 national ranking. He won bowl games

John Robinson with quarterback Sean Salisbury

ROBINSON AT USC

YEAR	RECORD (CONFERENCE)	BOWL
1976	11–1 (7–0, 1st)	Rose
1977	8–4 (5–2, T 2nd)	Bluebonnet
1978*	12–1 (6–1, 1st)	Rose
1979*	11–0–1 (6–0–1, 1st)	Rose
1980	8–2–1 (4–2–1, 3rd)	
1981	9–3 (5–2, T 2nd)	Fiesta
1982	8–3 (5–2, T 3rd)	
1993	8–5 (6–2, T 1st)	Freedom
1994	8–3–1 (6–2, T 2nd)	Cotton
1995	9–2–1, 6–1–1, T 1st)	Rose
1996	6–6 (3–5, T 5th)	
1997	6–5 (4–4, T 5th)	

*national champions

in each of his first four seasons, including three Rose Bowls.

During his first go-around at USC, before leaving to coach the Los Angeles Rams in 1983, Robinson posted a record of 11–3 against the school's archrivals. He was 6–1 against Notre Dame and 5–2 against UCLA. He coached two Heisman Trophy winners—Charles White (1979) and Marcus Allen (1981).

In 1978 and 1979, he won partial national titles. Alabama was awarded the major portion of the 1978 championship despite the fact that Robinson's Trojans beat the Crimson Tide 24–14 at Legion Field in Birmingham. Alabama, that season. From 1978 through 1980, he guided USC to a then-school-record 28-game unbeaten streak. In 1979, he was named National Coach of the Year.

Pete Carroll

It didn't take Pete Carroll long to achieve legendary status as USC's coach. After posting a 6–6 mark in his first year, the Trojans' football fortunes took off. Just take a look at the accomplishments of the next four years, 2002–2005: a 48–4 record, a 34-game winning streak, four BCS bowl appearances, four AP top 4 finishes, four Pac-10 titles, two national titles. And the talent keeps pouring into the program in a veritable avalanche.

A 1973 graduate of the University of the Pacific, Carroll spent the previous 16 years of his coaching career before taking over at USC in the professional ranks. His most recent NFL job was as head coach of the New England Patriots for three years.

His record after five years at USC stands at 54–10 for a phenomenal winning percentage of .844. He reached the 50-win mark faster than any other coach in school history. He owns a league-record .875 winning percentage in Pac-10 games, at 35–5. Conference records his team currently enjoys are a

27-game home winning streak and a 23-game conference-game winning streak.

Under Carroll USC was ranked No. 1 in a record 33 consecutive AP polls. For the first time in history, Heisman Trophy winners have come from the same school in three out of four years (Carson Palmer in 2002, Matt Leinart in 2004 and Reggie Bush in 2005). And with Carroll at the controls, USC came within 19 seconds in the 2006 Rose Bowl of the first national title three-peat since the Associated Press began ranking teams in 1936.

CARROLL AT USC

YEAR	RECORD (CONFERENCE)	BOWL
2001	6–6 (5–3, 5th)	Las Vegas
2002	11–2 (7–1, T 1st)	Orange
2003*	12–1 (7–1, 1st)	Rose
2004**	13–0 (8–0, 1st)	Orange
2005	12–1 (8–0, 1st)	Rose

*national champions

**consensus national champions

Pete Carroll hoists the hardware after USC's 28–14 Rose Bowl win over Michigan on January 1, 2004.

Israel Ifeanyi (No. 55) celebrates the Trojans' 41–32 win over Northwestern in the 1996 Rose Bowl—USC's 20th triumph in the granddaddy of them all.

TROJAN SUPERLATIVES

USC football history is littered with moments of greatness—national championships won, great games played, superior individual efforts, memorable upsets and more. Here is a small sample of that record of achievement.

The National Championships

1928

The University of Southern California first broke into the national championship business in 1928, during the days of coach Howard Jones and his Thundering Herd. The Trojans played a no-frills brand of football in those days. Opponents knew what was coming yet rarely could stop it. The 1928 Stanford team, coached by Glenn "Pop" Warner, was being called the greatest team in history. That is, until November 3, when Jones's Trojans forced

five fumbles and shut out the Indians 10–0. USC had lost to Notre Dame in the schools' first two meetings, in 1926 and 1927. Then in 1928, the Trojans came out on top of the Irish for the first time, 27–14, as Trojan back Don Williams ran for 93 yards and passed for 111 yards and two touchdowns. Led by tackle Jesse Hibbs, end Garrett Arbelide and the backfield of Williams, Harry Edelson, Russ Saunders and Marshall Duffield, the 1928 Trojans held 10 opponents to 59 points combined.

USC's 21–12 win over Tulane in the Rose Bowl capped a national championship season for Howard Jones' Trojans.

1931

USC captured its first consensus national title in 1931. The Trojans stumbled out of the gate with a 13–7 loss to St. Mary's in the season opener, but coach Howard Jones offered no excuses. His Thundering Herd lived up to its unofficial moniker by rolling over the remaining 10 opponents by a combined score of 356–39, shutting out six of them. After USC vanquished Notre Dame 16–14 in South Bend on what sportswriter Maxwell Stiles called "Johnny Baker's 10 little toes and three BIG points," a throng of more than 300,000 welcomed the Trojans back home to Los Angeles.

The Irish led 14–0 entering the fourth quarter, but the running of Gus Shaver and Orv Mohler and Baker's 33-yard field goal with one minute remaining keyed the victory that ended Notre Dame's 26-game unbeaten streak. In the regular-season finale, USC annihilated Georgia 60–0, after which Bulldog coach Harry Mehre called the 1931 Trojans "the greatest team I have ever seen." Jones stepped out of character and agreed, calling his team "the greatest offensive machine I have ever coached." The campaign ended with a 21–12 win over Tulane in the Rose Bowl. Four of the 1931 Trojans—Shaver, Baker, center Stan Williamson and halfback Erny Pinckert—were All-Americans.

The 1932 Trojans put an exclamation point on a dominant season with a 35-0 waxing of undefeated Pittsburgh in the Rose Bowl.

1932

The 1932 Thundering Herd repeated as consensus national champions with a trio of All-Americans—tackles Tay Brown and Ernie Smith and guard Aaron Rosenberg—and immortal quarterback Cotton Warburton leading the way. This was the peak of the Howard Jones era at USC. The Trojans finished the season 10–0 and riding a 20-game winning streak that was eventually extended to 25 games by midseason 1933. Jones had to replace most of his lineup, including All-Americans Gus Shaver, Erny Pinckert and Johnny Baker, from the 1931 title campaign, but by season's end, Jones's 1932 club was being hailed as his best ever. Indeed, it is recognized as one of the greatest football teams of all time. The Trojan line was virtually impenetrable, and it showed in the final results—13 points surrendered all season long, five straight shutout wins to start the season, a 13–0 blanking of Notre Dame to end the regular season and a 35–0 burial of undefeated Pittsburgh and coach Jock Sutherland in the Rose Bowl.

1939

This was the fourth national title of the Thundering Herd era, the second-to-last Trojan team coached by Howard Jones. The regular season began with a tie (7–7 against Oregon) and ended with a tie (0–0 against UCLA). Otherwise these Trojans were perfect. As usual, the defense was magnificent, pitching six shutouts and allowing only 33 points all year. Led by quarterback Grenny Lansdell and guard Harry Smith, the Trojans defeated highly ranked Oregon State 19–7 in Portland and three weeks later escaped the cold at Notre Dame with a 20–12 victory. USC's opponent in the Rose Bowl was Tennessee, under coach Bob Neyland. The Volunteers came into the contest riding a 23-game winning streak. They hadn't been scored on in 16 straight games. But the Trojans prevailed on that New Year's Day, 14–0.

1962

In 1962, John McKay coached USC to its first national championship in 23 years, and a dynasty was born. The 1962 Trojans fielded a two-man quarterback platoon of Pete Beathard and Bill Nelson, who between them combined for 18 touchdown passes and only three interceptions. All-America end Hal Bedsole was on the receiving end of 11 of those scoring tosses. He averaged 25.1 yards on 33 catches for the season. Tailback U was just beginning to earn its reputation, with Willie Brown averaging a robust 6.5 yards per carry in 1962. He led the team in rushing, interceptions, punt returns and kick returns and finished second to Bedsole in receptions. Another key member of the squad was guard-linebacker Damon Bame, who picked off four enemy aerials for the 1962 champs. Only 92 points were surrendered all year, and a 25–0 whitewashing of Notre Dame was one of three shutout wins.

1967

The second national title of the John McKay era at USC came courtesy of the star-studded 1967 club. Tailback O.J. Simpson set a school record (which he broke the following season) with 1,543 rushing yards and 13 touchdowns, averaging 5.3 per carry. Simpson went on to capture the 1968 Heisman Trophy.

Quarterback Steve Sogge added 1,032 passing yards with seven touchdown tosses. Leading the way for the attack was 1967 Outland Trophy recipient Ron Yary at tackle. The defense boasted a pair of All-Americans in end Tim Rossovich and linebacker Adrian Young.

The only blemish on the record was a 3–0 loss in the rain and mud at Oregon State. The key midseason matchup was a 24–7 win over defending national champion Notre Dame, a game in which Young registered a school-record four interceptions. In the regular-season finale, the Trojans, ranked fourth nationally, defeated top-ranked UCLA and Heisman Trophy winner Gary Beban, 21–20. Simpson's 64-yard run to win the game is one of the most unforgettable moments in football history. Five Trojans were selected in the first round of the 1968 NFL Draft, and Yary went first overall.

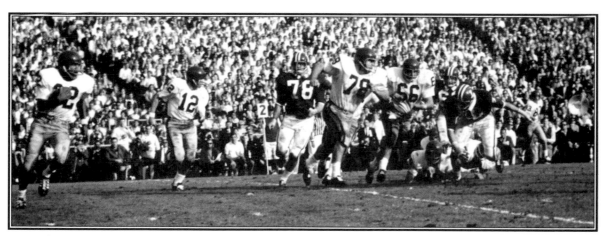

O.J. Simpson and the national champion Trojans earned a 14–3 win over Indiana in the 1968 Rose Bowl.

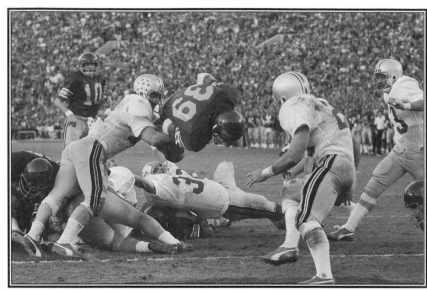

Fullback Sam Cunningham (No. 39) dives into the end zone for his fourth touchdown against Ohio State in the 1973 Rose Bowl.

1972

The 1972 Trojans, with John McKay still at the helm, were as dominant a team as there has ever been. They were never seriously challenged. Senior Mike Rae and sophomore Pat Haden doubled up on the quarterback duties; All-America tight end Charles Young led the Trojan receivers with 29 catches, three for scores, averaging 16.5 yards per grab; and wide receiver Lynn Swann averaged 21 yards on 26 receptions. Tailback Anthony Davis paced the ground game with 1,191 yards, despite not starting until the eighth game, and averaged 5.8 per carry. Fullback Sam "Bam" Cunningham

was unstoppable in short-yardage situations, especially near the goal line. On defense, tackle John Grant and linebacker Richard Wood were first-team All-Americans. Wood racked up 129 tackles that fall. The 1972 Trojans beat fourth-ranked Arkansas 31–10 and 10th-ranked Notre Dame 45–23 during the regular season, then whipped Ohio State 42–17 in the Rose Bowl. The 1972 team, the best of the John McKay era, was anointed national champion by unanimous acclaim. Like Howard Jones's 1932 Thundering Herd, any talk of the greatest teams of all time that does not include the immortal 1972 Trojans is of no interest.

1974

In 1974, tailback Anthony Davis was an All-American, and linebacker Richard Wood became USC's first three-year All-American. A loss to Arkansas in War Memorial Stadium in Little Rock in the season opener and a 15–15 midseason tie with California marred the record, but the voters in several selection boards saw this Trojan team as the nation's best. Davis was runner-up for the Heisman Trophy after rushing for 1,421 yards and 13 touchdowns, and he left USC in possession of Pac-8 records for career rushing yards (3,724) and touchdowns (52). He scored four touchdowns in USC's unbelievable 55–24 comeback win over Notre Dame in 1974, bringing his career touchdown total against the Irish to 11. Pat Haden threw 13 touchdown passes, a school record at the time, for the second straight year. In the 18–17 Rose Bowl win over Ohio State to conclude the 1974 campaign, Haden won the game with a 38-yard touchdown strike to J.K. McKay and the subsequent two-point conversion to Shelton Diggs with two minutes remaining in the game. For the third year in a row, five Trojan players were All-Americans. In addition to Davis and Wood were tight end Jim Obradovich, guard Bill Bain and defensive back Charles Phillips.

1978

The UPI named USC national champion following the 1978 season. The AP picked Alabama, despite the fact that John Robinson's Trojans beat Bear Bryant's Crimson Tide 24–14 at Legion Field in Birmingham, Alabama on September 23. The only blemish on the record was a 20–7 loss at Arizona State. All-America tailback Charles White became the Pac-10's career rushing leader, and he was still a junior. His 1,859 yards in 1978 were just a taste of the 2,000-yard-plus campaign to come the following year. Marcus Allen was White's backup. Paul McDonald threw for 1,690 yards to lead the conference, and his 19 touchdown passes set a school record. Flanker Kevin Williams was on the receiving end of 10 touchdown passes. The offensive line featured two of the all-time greats in Brad Budde and Anthony Munoz, in addition to All-American Pat Howell. On defense, Dennis Smith and Ronnie Lott roamed the deep zones. Late in the season, the Trojans edged defending national champion Notre Dame 27–25. A 17–10 Rose Bowl win over Michigan capped off the season.

2003

With Pete Carroll at the controls, USC found new life and won a national title after a quarter-century hiatus. Carroll had to replace Heisman Trophy winner Carson Palmer at quarterback and All-America safety Troy Polamalu, among a host of other stars, and came back even stronger. After a 34–31 loss at California in three overtimes, the Trojans would not lose a single one of their next 34 games. USC served notice on the rest of the football world in the 2003 opener with a 23–0 drubbing of an Auburn Tiger team that many believed to be a good bet to win the national title. The game was at Auburn, and it wasn't as close as the score. The 2003 Trojans set Pac-10 records by scoring 30 points in each of 11 straight games, and 40 points in seven in a row. They swept traditional rivals UCLA and Notre Dame for the second straight year for only the second time in history. The festivities came to an end with a seemingly routine 28–14 win over fourth-ranked Michigan in the Rose Bowl. Quarterback Matt Leinart, wide receiver Mike Williams, offensive tackle Jacob Rogers, defensive end Kenechi Udeze and punter Tom Malone were All-Americans. Leinart had never thrown a pass in a college game before 2003, and he was named Pac-10 Offensive Player of the Year. LenDale White ran for 754 yards and became the first freshman ever to lead the Trojans in rushing. Hershel Dennis and Reggie Bush joined White in a three-man tailback rotation. There were two future Heisman Trophy winners—Leinart and Bush—at USC in 2003.

Darnell Bing (No. 20) and Brandon Hance (No. 8) celebrate during the second quarter of the 2004 Rose Bowl.

LenDale White dives into the end zone in USC's 55–19 Orange Bowl rout of Oklahoma.

2004

The motto of the 2004 USC football team was "Leave no doubt." Leinart, Bush and White all returned, and the Trojans sailed to 13–0. The defense was populated by four All-Americans—tackles Shaun Cody and Mike Patterson and linebackers Matt Grootegoed and Lofa Tatupu—and finished in the top 10 nationally in all major defensive statistical categories, including first in rushing defense and third in scoring defense. USC outscored its opponents by 25.2 points per game, including a school-record eight games with a margin of victory of 30 or more points. The Men of Troy opened 2004 with a 24–13 win over Virginia Tech at a neutral site. Before midseason came wins over seventh-ranked California and 15th-ranked Arizona State on consecutive weekends. On November 27, USC gave Notre Dame a 31-point drubbing for the third year in a row, with a 29–24 win over crosstown rival UCLA to conclude the regular season. On January 4, the Trojans annihilated second-ranked Oklahoma 55–19 in the Orange Bowl, leaving no doubt. The winning streak stood at 22.

CONFERENCE CHAMPIONSHIPS

YEAR	CONFERENCE	OVERALL
1927*	4–0–1 (Pacific Coast)	8–1–1
1928	4–0–1 (Pacific Coast)	9–0–1
1929	6–1 (Pacific Coast)	10–2
1931	7–0 (Pacific Coast)	10–1
1932	6–0 (Pacific Coast)	10–0
1938*	6–1 (Pacific Coast)	9–2
1939*	5–0–2 (Pacific Coast)	8–0–2
1943	5–0 (Pacific Coast)	8–2
1944	3–0–2 (Pacific Coast)	8–0–2
1945	5–1 (Pacific Coast)	7–4
1947	6–0 (Pacific Coast)	7–2–1
1952	6–0 (Pacific Coast)	10–1
1954	6–1 (Pacific Coast)	8–4
1959*	3–1 (Pacific Coast)	8–2
1962	4–0 (Pacific Coast)	11–0
1964*	3–1 (Pac-8)	7–3
1966	4–1 (Pac-8)	7–4
1967	6–1 (Pac-8)	10–1

YEAR	CONFERENCE	OVERALL
1968	6–0 (Pac-8)	9–1–1
1969	6–0 (Pac-8)	10–0–1
1972	7–0 (Pac-8)	12–0
1973	7–0 (Pac-8)	9–2–1
1974	6–0–1 (Pac-8)	10–1–1
1976	7–0 (Pac-8)	11–1
1978	6–1 (Pac-10)	12–1
1979	6–0–1 (Pac-10)	11–0–1
1984	7–1 (Pac-10)	9–3
1987*	7–1 (Pac-10)	8–4
1988	8–0 (Pac-10)	10–2
1989	6 0–1 (Pac-10)	9–2–1
1993*	6–2 (Pac-10)	8–5
2002*	7–1 (Pac-10)	11–2
2003	7–1 (Pac-10)	12–1
2004	8–0 (Pac-10)	13–0
2005	8–0 (Pac-10)	12–1

*co-championships

John McKay (right) jokes with University of Wisconsin football coach Milt Bruhn less than two weeks after USC beat Wisconsin, 42–37, in the 1963 Rose Bowl.

The Greatest Games

USC 42, WISCONSIN 37
JANUARY 1, 1963

The 1963 Rose Bowl matched No. 1–ranked USC against No. 2 Wisconsin. Quarterback Pete Beathard passed the Trojans to a 21–7 lead by halftime and extended it to 28–7 early in the third period. Wisconsin quarterback Ron Vander Kelen scampered 17 yards for a score to cut the Trojan lead to 28–14. Two Beathard touchdown passes later, the Trojans held a 42–14 lead. But behind Vander Kelen the Badgers stormed back in the fourth quarter, scoring 23 unanswered points. They scored two touchdowns in three minutes, then a botched USC punt snap resulted in a safety. Three plays after the free kick, Vander Kelen found receiver Pat Richter with a 19-yard touchdown pass with 1:19 remaining. The Trojans recovered the onside kick and won the hard-fought battle 42–37. The prize was the 1962 national title, USC's first in 23 years and the first of four in the John McKay coaching era. Vander Kelen threw for a Rose Bowl– and Wisconsin-record 401 yards in a losing effort, and Richter caught 11 passes for 163 yards. Beathard threw four touchdown passes for the Trojans. The 79 combined points set a Rose Bowl record that stood for 28 years.

"We're still No. 1, and they're still No. 2. They're a good team, but they'd finish about sixth in our league." —JOHN MCKAY, A LITTLE MIFFED THAT THE FINAL SCORE OF THE 1963 ROSE BOWL WAS SO CLOSE

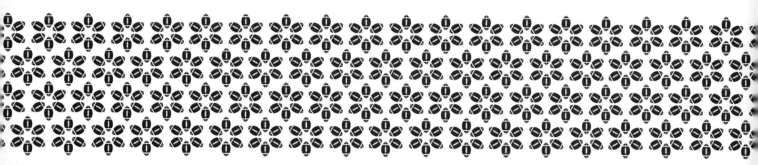

USC 20, NOTRE DAME 17
NOVEMBER 28, 1964

Notre Dame finished the 1963 season 2–7, then hired Northwestern coach Ara Parseghian to resurrect the program. In Parseghian's first year, 1964, the Irish were 9–0, ranked No. 1 and headed out to the L.A. Coliseum for their annual clash with USC. It would be their 10th win against no losses and the icing on a national title cake. But coach John McKay and his Trojans had other ideas. It wasn't McKay's best team, but it was 6–3 and had secured a tie for the conference title.

Irish quarterback John Huarte, who would win the Heisman Trophy that year,

connected with receiver Jack Snow time and time again in the first half, and the visitors led 17–0 at the intermission. But the Trojans came storming back, taking the second-half kickoff and marching 66 yards down the field, culminating in a Mike Garrett touchdown run. When quarterback Craig Fertig hit Fred Hill with a touchdown pass, the Trojans had pulled within four points. Irish hearts were broken when Fertig found halfback Rod Sherman in the end zone with 1:33 to play for the 20–17 win. The Trojan victory cost Notre Dame the national championship.

Mike Garrett and John McKay celebrate one of the most memorable and gratifying wins in USC history—a 20-17 win over top-ranked Notre Dame after trailing 17-0 at halftime.

O.J. Simpson completes one of the signature plays in USC history—his 64-yard touchdown run against UCLA.

RED-23 BLAST
USC 21, UCLA 20
NOVEMBER 18, 1967

The Rose Bowl was the prize when fourth-ranked USC, with former junior college phenom O.J. Simpson at tailback, and top-ranked UCLA, with Heisman Trophy winner Gary Beban at quarterback, clashed in 1967. Beban threw for 301 yards that day despite a painful rib injury. Simpson ran for two touchdowns. One was for 13 yards, dramatizing his power as he broke half a dozen tackles. "I was

hit several times," Simpson said. "I was surprised to score." Simpson's legendary 64-yard run with 10:38 remaining in the fourth quarter won the game 21–20 and put coach John McKay's Trojans in the Rose Bowl.

The score was tied at 14 early in the fourth quarter when Beban connected with Dave Nuttall on a 20-yard touchdown pass to give the Bruins the lead. But the Trojans blocked the extra-point attempt and the score stood at 20–14. USC coach John McKay replaced quarterback Steve Sogge with Toby Page, a better passer. But with third-and-eight at the USC 36 and a pass play called, Page saw the UCLA linebackers drop back into pass coverage and audibled into a Red-23 Blast. What happened next made college football history.

Simpson's run left the crowd of 90,772 at the Coliseum dazzled, all but disbelieving. O.J. later told *Los Angeles Times* sportswriter Mal Florence:

> On third-and-eight, my fullback, Danny Scott, blew through the hole, and I was right behind him. My only thought was that I needed eight yards to get a first down. Scott popped [UCLA linebacker Don] Manning at what would have been the first-down marker. I hopped over Manning, and then I jumped outside.

> I was on the sideline, and I felt that if I could get back to the middle of the field, I might be able to outrun [everybody] to the end zone. So I just cut to the middle, got by a couple of guys, and our Earl McCullouch was making a screening block on [safety Sandy] Green. At that point it was just a race to the end zone, and when I got there, I was exhausted. I dropped the ball, but I couldn't stop as my legs carried me another 10 or 15 yards.

That unforgettable run gave Southern California the Pac-8 title and a berth in the Rose Bowl, where the Trojans beat Indiana 14–3 and won the national championship.

"THE COMEBACK"
USC 55, NOTRE DAME 24
NOVEMBER 30, 1974

One of the most memorable college football games to come out of the 1970s was Southern California's 55–24 trouncing of Notre Dame, which led 24–0 at one point and 24–6 at halftime. Against what was ranked the nation's strongest defense before that game on November 30, 1974, in the Los Angeles Coliseum, the Trojans ran up 55 points in a span of 17 minutes. It was incredible, fantastic, almost beyond comprehension.

That was the day Anthony Davis scored four touchdowns against the Irish. He had made six touchdowns against them in 1972 and one in 1973, plus a two-point conversion for a total of 68 points.

"Gentlemen, we're not playing too well," Trojans coach John McKay said at halftime, carefully keeping his emotions in check. He

reminded his players that his 1964 team had fought back from a 17–0 deficit to win 20–17. He insisted they could do it, too.

Remembering that Davis had returned two Notre Dame kickoffs for touchdowns of 97 and 96 yards in 1972, the Irish hadn't kicked to Davis in the first half in 1974. But McKay predicted that the third-quarter kickoff would go to Davis and added that he would come back a long way with it.

Davis, interviewed by Mel Florence of the *Los Angeles Times*, said: "I looked at [linebacker] Richard Wood and he looked at me and we said, 'This man has lost his mind.' Then, I'm walking out of the locker room and I'm about 50 yards ahead of the Notre Dame team and somebody yelled out, 'We're going to kick the ball to Davis, and we're going to kick his ———.'"

What did Davis do but return the second-half kickoff 102 yards. And a rout was on.

Anthony Davis was the ultimate ND-killer, scoring 11 touchdowns in three games against the Irish, including four in the epic 55–24 comeback win.

The Trojans first got on the scoreboard on a seven-yard pass from Pat Haden to Davis with 10 seconds left before halftime, but the two-point-conversion attempt failed and the second half began with the Irish up 24–6. Then USC scored 35 points in the third quarter, with Davis opening the floodgates on the kickoff, adding two more scores on short runs, and Haden finding J.K. McKay on scoring passes of 18 and 45 yards. Then, within the first two minutes of the fourth quarter, Haden hit Shelton Diggs on a 16-yard scoring toss and Charles Phillips returned an interception 58 yards for a touchdown to close the book on the 55–24 blitzkrieg.

In Davis's own words: "We turned into madmen."

Jim Obradovich leaps into the air to catch a pass in front of OSU's Tim Fox in the 1975 Rose Bowl.

USC 18, OHIO STATE 17
JANUARY 1, 1975

The 1975 Rose Bowl was billed as a matchup of the two most exciting running backs in the nation—USC's Anthony Davis and Ohio State's Archie Griffin. But when the second-ranked Buckeyes and fourth-ranked Trojans squared off in Pasadena, the expected extravaganza never materialized. The Trojans held Griffin, who had just won the first of his two Heisman Trophies, to 75 rushing yards. Davis left the game with an injury after picking up 67 yards. USC drew first blood with a 30-yard field goal in the first quarter, but the Buckeyes took a 7–3 lead into the halftime break after a two-yard touchdown run by Harold Henson. After a scoreless third quarter, the Trojans retook the lead on an eight-yard pass from quarterback Pat Haden to tight end Jim Obradovich in the fourth. But the Buckeyes scored on their first two possessions of the final stanza. Quarterback Cornelius Greene piloted an 82-yard drive and took it in for the score himself from three yards out, and a 32-yard Tom Klaban field goal made it 17–10 Ohio State. Haden then drove the Trojans 83 yards down the field and hit wide receiver J.K. McKay with a 38-yard touchdown pass to bring the score to 17–16 with just over two minutes to play. Coach John McKay gambled and decided to go for the win. Haden drilled a pass to a diving Shelton Diggs in the end zone for the two-point conversion. McKay's gamble paid off in a big way with his club winning the national title as voted by the coaches in the UPI poll.

USC 24, ALABAMA 14
SEPTEMBER 23, 1978

In 1977, Bear Bryant's Crimson Tide put an end to USC's 15-game winning streak with a 21–20 win in Los Angeles. The following year on September 23 the two teams met again at Legion Field in Birmingham, Alabama, with more than 77,000 in attendance and a national television audience watching at home. Alabama sat atop the national polls at No. 1 and was a 14-point favorite over the seventh-ranked Trojans.

USC tailback Charles White was custodian of his school's reputation as Tailback U. He had run for 1,478 yards in 1977 and was at work on an 1,859-yard 1978. Left-handed quarterback Paul McDonald was a pinpoint passer for the Men of Troy. The Trojans took control of the game in the first half, winning the battle in the trenches. White fumbled the ball away on the Bama 2-yard line in the first quarter, but he redeemed himself on USC's next possession with a 40-yard touchdown run around right end.

Tide quarterback Jeff Rutledge and running back Major Ogilvie were unable to move the ball at all in the first half against the stubborn Trojan defense. USC put together a nine-minute, 23-play drive in the second quarter that ended in a field goal and a 10–0 halftime lead.

In the third quarter, Ogilvie scored on a 41-yard run, bringing the Tide to within three points. But the Trojans answered right back, with White doing most of the damage on the ground. Then, from the Bama 6, McDonald hit flanker Kevin Williams with a scoring toss for a 17–7 lead and extended it to 24–7 in the fourth quarter with a 40-yard touchdown pass to Williams.

Alabama found pay dirt one more time on a 41-yard pass from Rutledge to Barry Krauss, but the Trojan defense held firm the rest of the way, and USC returned home to L.A. as 24–14 winners.

USC 17, OHIO STATE 16
JANUARY 1, 1980

Five years earlier, USC scored a one-point victory, 18–17, over Ohio State in the 1975 Rose Bowl. On New Year's Day, 1980, history repeated itself almost verbatim.

The 1979 Ohio State team began the season unranked and with modest expectations, but the Buckeyes went 11-0 and entered

Chip Baker (No. 51) makes a grab for OSU quarterback Art Schlichter (No. 10) during the third quarter of the 1980 Rose Bowl.

the 1980 Rose Bowl as Big Ten champions. The Trojans also entered the contest undefeated, with only a tie against Stanford to mar the record. USC tailback Charles White, who had picked up his Heisman Trophy just weeks earlier, made the game his personal showcase, rushing for a Rose Bowl–record 247 yards. But the Buckeyes made it interesting.

The Trojans took a 10–0 lead on a 41-yard Eric Hipp field goal in the first quarter and a 53-yard pass from Paul McDonald to Kevin Williams in the second. But the Buckeyes made it 10-all before halftime on a Vlade Janakievski field goal from 35 yards out and a 53-yard pass from Art Schlichter to Gary Williams. Ohio State led 16–10 in the fourth quarter thanks to two more Janakievski three-pointers. With 5:21 left to play, USC took possession of the ball at its own 17 yard line, and White took over the game. The Trojans marched down the field, exclusively on the ground. White himself accounted for 71 of the 83 yards and won the game by diving in from one yard out.

USC 55, OKLAHOMA 19
JANUARY 4, 2005

It wasn't a very competitive game, but for a statement, it slammed the door on any doubters. Indeed, the motto of the 2004 USC team was "Leave No Doubt," a result of having been excluded from the 2003 BCS championship game. The Associated Press had proclaimed the 2003 Trojans national champions, and even though the American Football Coaches Association instructs its members to vote the winner of the BCS title game (LSU following the 2003 season) No. 1 in their final poll, three of them voted for USC anyway. But the absence of official BCS verification left doubts in the minds of some fans and media, and the 2004 Trojans were on a mission to rectify the situation.

USC entered the 2005 Orange Bowl, the official verification for the 2004 season, 12–0, riding a 21-game winning streak and ranked No. 1 in the nation. Oklahoma was 12–0 and ranked second. Four of the 2004 Heisman Trophy finalists—USC's Matt Leinart and Reggie Bush and Oklahoma's Jason White and Adrian Peterson—participated in the contest.

There were 77,912 in the stands at Miami's Pro Player Stadium and a prime-time ABC TV audience looking on.

The Sooners looked like they might make a game of it early, drawing first blood on a five-yard touchdown pass from White to Travis Wilson to cap off a 92-yard drive. But the Trojans rebounded with 28 unanswered points. Before the first quarter ended, they had gone up 14–7 on a 33-yard touchdown pass from Leinart to Dominique Byrd and a six-yard LenDale White touchdown run. In the second quarter, USC added two more Leinart touchdown passes (54 yards to Dwayne Jarrett and five yards to Steve Smith) to take a 28–7 lead before the Sooners knew what hit them.

Garrett Hartley knocked a 29-yard field goal through for OU to make it 28–10, but the Trojans made it 38–10 at the half on a 33-yard Leinart-to-Smith TD pass and a 33-yard Ryan Killeen field goal. In the third quarter, Leinart tacked on his Orange Bowl-record and school-record tying fifth touchdown pass (four yards to Smith, for his school-record-tying third touchdown catch), and Killeen connected on another three-pointer from 42 yards out to

Dominique Byrd's acrobatic touchdown grab opened the floodgates in USC's 55–19 demolition of Oklahoma.

makc it 48–10. Early in the fourth quarter, LenDale White scored from the Oklahoma 8, and from there the Trojans coasted to a 55–19 no-doubter.

USC accumulated 525 total yards, averaging an amazing 8.3 yards per play, and rang up a school record with its eighth win by 30 or more points in one season. With the victory, USC repeated as national champion and became just the second team ever to hold the No. 1 spot in the AP rankings from preseason through the final poll.

USC 34, NOTRE DAME 31
OCTOBER 15, 2005

For as long as fans discuss the greatest football games of all time, the 2005 Southern California–Notre Dame game will be a part of the dialogue. It was one game that lived up to the overwhelming hype leading up to it. ESPN's *Game Day* telecast originated from the Notre Dame campus that day, and NBC televised the contest to a national audience. After warming up in their familiar gold and blue uniforms, the Irish players emerged from the tunnel in Kelly green jerseys. What the Trojans had going for them that the Fighting Irish didn't was two Heisman Trophy winners—quarterback Matt Leinart (2004) and tailback Reggie Bush (2005).

Leinart threw for 301 yards, but all five Trojan touchdowns came via the ground game. Bush streaked 36 yards for a first-quarter touchdown to open the scoring. But the Irish answered quickly with a 16-yard scoring run, moments after converting a fourth-and-one from their own 29 to keep the drive alive. Still in the first quarter, Leinart found tight end Dominique Byrd with a 52-yard pass, and two

plays later LenDale White scored from three yards out to put USC up 14–7.

Notre Dame scored twice in the second quarter on a 32-yard pass from Brady Quinn to Jeff Samardzija and a 60-yard punt return by Tom Zbikowski and led 21–14 at halftime. The only points in the third quarter came on a 45-yard run by Bush, knotting the score at 21.

The fourth quarter treated college football fandom to some unbelievable drama. First, D.J. Fitzpatrick put the home team up 24–21 with a 32-yard field goal. The Trojans went ahead 28–24 on Bush's nine-yard burst, his career-best third touchdown run of the game. The Irish drove down the field to the USC 5, and Quinn scored around right end from there to give ND a 31–28 lead with 3:05 left to play.

That was way too much time for these Trojans. For a moment they appeared to run out of ideas, but Leinart came through with perhaps the greatest heroics of his illustrious college career—twice in the same drive. With his team facing fourth-and-nine from its own 26, he launched a beautiful pass to wide receiver Dwayne Jarrett for 61 yards to the Irish 13, deflating the frenzied crowd of

Reggie Bush outruns Notre Dame defenders on his way to a third-quarter touchdown.

80,795 in attendance. Four plays later, with the ball on the Notre Dame 2, Leinart darted around left end and leapt toward the flag, but the ball was knocked out of his hands and out of bounds at the Irish 1. The clock mistakenly ran down to 0:00, whereupon the crowd began to storm the field. After a conference by the officials, seven seconds were restored, the field was cleared and the ball was spotted for the next play. With no timeouts remaining, coach Pete Carroll signaled to Leinart to spike the ball, most likely for a game-tying field goal and overtime. But Leinart was having none of it; with no timeouts, he twisted and spun into the end zone with three seconds left.

Notre Dame had possession of the ball almost twice as long as USC (38:40 to 21:20), but the Trojans outgained the Irish by 476 yards to 417 and outscored them 34–31.

THE RIVALRIES

Two great rivalries have helped define USC football and have given fans many of their greatest memories. One of them happens to be the greatest intersectional rivalry in all of football.

—————— USC-Notre Dame ——————

Beginning on Sunday, October 16, 2005, sportswriters and fans began to speak of the previous day's USC–Notre Dame football game as perhaps the greatest of all time. By the time the final gun sounded, not one player who participated in the contest had anything left to give. First-year Fighting Irish coach Charlie Weis wanted no part of the "greatest game of all time" dialogue—he was the losing coach in a football game, and that's all that mattered to him. But two Trojan Heisman Trophy winners—quarterback Matt Leinart and running back Reggie Bush—were almost too exhausted to talk. Leinart was visibly shaken by what he had just experienced, and by the Herculean effort it took to prevail over the Irish and keep USC's win streak alive, extending it to 28 games. Best game ever or not, it was one for the ages.

There is something special about the Southern California–Notre Dame series, the oldest and most prestigious intersectional rivalry in the country. Over the years, many national championships have been certified or lost based on the outcome of the matchup that first occurred in 1926. The 77-game series has been replete with improbable endings, individual accomplishments and controversial plays.

It's a game that has enhanced the candidacy of Heisman Trophy winners. For USC the names are Mike Garrett, O.J. Simpson, Charles White, Marcus Allen, Carson Palmer, Leinart and Bush.

It's a game that has matched the skill and knowledge of famous and legendary coaches: USC's Howard Jones, John McKay and John Robinson and Notre Dame's Knute Rockne, Frank Leahy and Ara Parseghian.

It's a game that attracted the largest crowd in the history of college football, an estimated 120,000 for the 1927 meeting at Soldier Field in Chicago. The 1947 game at the Los Angeles Coliseum drew 104,953, still a record for that venerable stadium.

Yet, if it hadn't been for the persuasiveness of the bride of a young USC graduate manager and the wife of an immortal coach, there might not have been a Notre Dame–Southern California rivalry.

In 1925, Notre Dame was already an established college football power under Rockne. On January 1 that year, the Fighting Irish with the Four Horsemen had galloped over Stanford 27–10 in the Rose Bowl game. USC had emerged in the 1920s as a formidable football force on the West Coast, but was not recognized nationally.

Gwynn Wilson, USC's graduate manager of athletics at the time, recalled the unique circumstances that resulted in the start of the storied series.

"I knew that Notre Dame was going to break its series with Nebraska (after the 1925 game) and that there would be an opening on its schedule," Wilson said. "Notre Dame was to play Nebraska on Thanksgiving Day, and I thought if I went back there and talked to Rockne, there might be a chance for us to get a game with them next year."

Wilson had an ally in Jones, who had been hired in 1925 and wanted to make a national impact. While coaching at Iowa in 1921, his

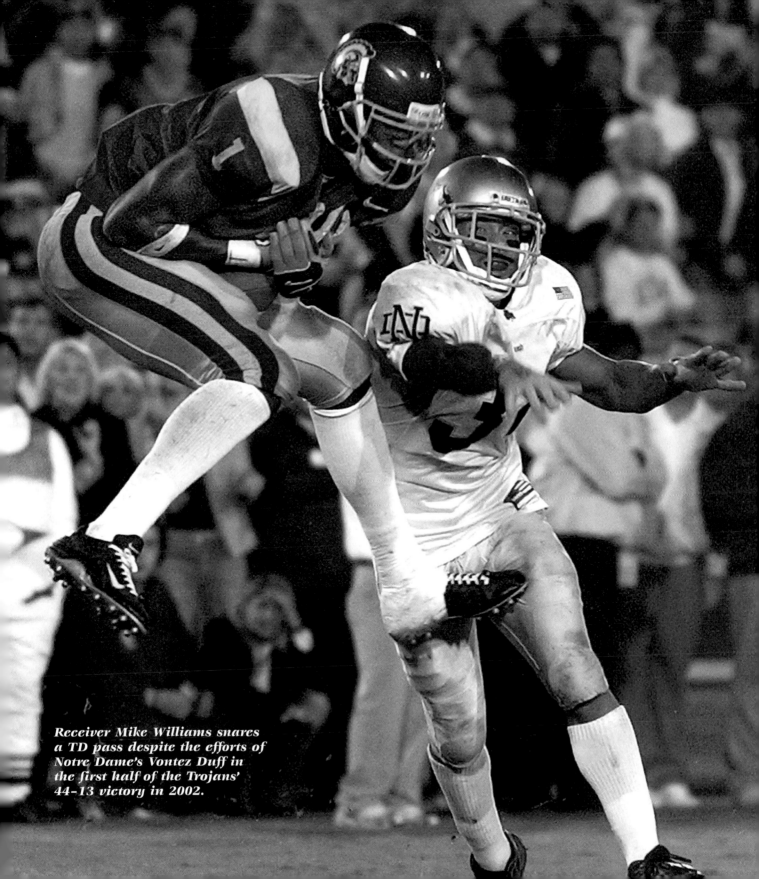

Receiver Mike Williams snares a TD pass despite the efforts of Notre Dame's Vontez Duff in the first half of the Trojans' 44-13 victory in 2002.

Matt Grootegoed (No. 6) and Dallas Sartz (No. 42) drag down Notre Dame's Marcus Wilson during USC's 41–10 win over the Irish on November 27, 2004.

team had snapped a 22-game Notre Dame unbeaten streak. He had agreed to give Rockne a rematch sometime. It wouldn't be at Iowa, though.

It was Wilson's notion to establish a home-and-home series with the Irish. However, he had to convince Harold Stonier, who was USC's executive secretary and number two man in the administration.

Wilson didn't have to do much convincing, because Stonier believed it was about time that USC, then a growing university, should try to become nationally prominent in football.

USC had played few intersectional games, the most notable being a 14–3 win over Penn State in the Rose Bowl in 1923, and hadn't traveled east.

Stonier agreed to Wilson's plan to meet Rockne, but the 26-year-old graduate manager had still another request.

"I asked Harold if it would be all right to take my wife along, because we had been married only six months," Wilson said. "Those things weren't being done in those days. We didn't have big expense accounts, but Stonier agreed."

So Wilson and his bride, Marion, took Southern Pacific's Sunset Limited to Lincoln and a rendezvous with Rockne.

"I went to the hotel where the Notre Dame team was staying, but Rockne told me he didn't have enough time to talk about my proposal there," Wilson said. "He said he'd get a ticket to Chicago for me and my wife and he'd talk to me about it on the train."

It didn't help Wilson's cause that Notre Dame was shut out by Nebraska 17–0. Nonetheless, the Wilsons were still hopeful. Wilson said:

I really didn't get a chance to talk to Rockne until the afternoon after the game, when we went into the observation car. He told me that he couldn't meet Southern Cal because Notre Dame was already traveling too much, and the team had gotten the nickname of Ramblers, which he didn't like. He also said he was now getting some games with the Big Ten.

I thought the whole thing was off, but as Rock and I talked, Marion was with Mrs. Rockne, Bonnie, in her compartment. Marion told Bonnie how nice Southern California was and how hospitable the people were.

Well, when Rock went back to the compartment, Bonnie talked him into the game. He came out, looked me up and said, 'What kind of proposition do you have?' I said, 'We'll give you a $20,000 guarantee.' He said he would talk to Father Matthew J. Walsh [Notre Dame president]. He did, and the series was on, with the first game to be played on December 4, 1926.

But if it hadn't been for Mrs. Wilson talking to Mrs. Rockne, there wouldn't have been a series.

Rockne was with his team when it traveled by train to Los Angeles, working out twice along the way, for the first meeting with USC.

The Trojans were as formidable as the Irish with an 8–1 record, having lost only to Stanford, 13–12.

The teams had contrasting styles. Notre Dame employed a backfield shift and misdirection plays. USC was a single-wing power, tailback oriented. Jones's teams became known as the Thundering Herd.

A sellout crowd of 74,378 saw the game at the Coliseum, which was later enlarged for the 1932 Olympics. USC led 12–7 late in the game when Art Parisien found Butch Niemiec with a 23-yard touchdown pass.

USC center Jeff Cravath, who became the school's 12th coach 16 years later, blocked the extra-point try, but it was inconsequential as the Irish won the first game of the series 13–12.

Extra-point failures would haunt the Trojans in two of the next three meetings with Notre Dame. The Irish won 7–6 in 1927 and 13–12 in 1929 when Russ Saunders of the Trojans returned a kickoff 95 yards for a touchdown.

Rockne died March 31, 1931, in a plane crash in Kansas. Part of his legacy was the talented team that his successor, Hunk Anderson, inherited.

The Irish, riding a 26-game unbeaten streak that fall, were substantially favored over the Trojans, who had won six straight after opening the season with a 13–7 loss to St. Mary's.

It seemed that the odds were justified on a November afternoon in South Bend, Indiana. Notre Dame, behind the slashing running of Schwartz and Steve Banas, led 14–0 after three quarters.

That was a sizeable lead in those days, when passing skills weren't as refined as now. However, an incident that didn't seem relevant at the time altered the course of the game emotionally and tactically.

USC fullback Jim Musick suffered a broken nose after Notre Dame scored its second touchdown, in the third period, and was helped off the field. His Trojan teammates were incensed, charging unnecessarily rough play by the Irish. Orv Mohler replaced Musick, but not at fullback. Instead, he became the quarterback with Gus Shaver moving from quarterback to fullback.

That combination would prove to be devastating as the Trojans scored two touchdowns in the final period. However, guard Johnny Baker's extra-point attempt was blocked after the first touchdown. USC seemed destined to lose another one-point game to Notre Dame.

With time running out, another Trojan drive carried to the Notre Dame 15, where it stalled. Jones was concerned that Mohler wouldn't call for a field goal and sent in quarterback Homer Griffith for that purpose. Griffith was waved back to the bench by captain and center Stan Williamson. Mohler had already made up his mind and held the ball for Baker, whose field-goal try was perfect from the 23-yard line with one minute remaining. USC's unexpected 16–14 victory ranks with the most dramatic college games of all time.

One of the most unforgettable games in the modern era of the USC–Notre Dame series took place in 1964 at the Coliseum. USC, trailing 17–0 at halftime, deprived previously unbeaten Notre Dame of the national championship with a 20–17 victory on quarterback Craig Fertig's fourth-down pass to halfback Rod Sherman with 1:33 remaining. The outcome enabled Alabama to win the title. Crimson

Tide coach Bear Bryant showed his appreciation. He awarded Alabama letters to Fertig and Sherman. That made them the only players ever to receive letters from two different schools in the same season.

In the aftermath of that game, the Reverend Theodore Hesburgh, Notre Dame president from 1952 to 1987, congratulated McKay, saying, "That wasn't a very nice thing for a Catholic [McKay] to do."

Replied McKay, "Father, it serves you right for hiring a Presbyterian [Parseghian]."

For those who are intrigued by unaccountable turnabouts, the 1974 game before a crowd of 83,552 at the Coliseum was the most bizarre. Notre Dame was on the verge of routing favored USC with a 24–0 lead late in the second quarter. The Trojans scored just before halftime on a short pass from Pat Haden to Anthony Davis, making it 24–6, but it was regarded merely as a token touchdown of a beaten team.

However, Davis, who had scored six touchdowns against Notre Dame in 1972, when the Trojans won 45–23, returned the third-quarter

Justin Fargas splits Notre Dame defenders Courtney Watson (left) and Shane Walton for a 47-yard gain in the Trojans' win over the Irish in 2002.

kickoff 102 yards for a touchdown, one of his four on the day. Davis had brought back two 1972 kickoffs for touchdowns against the Irish. In three years, he scored 11 touchdowns against them.

That third-quarter TD had a catalytic effect. In one of the most astonishing periods ever played, the Trojans scored 35 points. They totaled 49 points in 17 minutes of the second half.

The Irish were dazed and routed 55–24 with most of the fourth quarter remaining. "We turned into madmen," said Davis.

In 1966, the Irish rolled 51–0 in L.A., with Coley O'Brien subbing for an injured Terry Hanratty at quarterback. It was the worst loss in USC history. In the following year, McKay constantly reviewed that game film in his darkened office, searching for clues.

"We finally had to burn it when he wasn't looking," said Fertig, then an assistant coach.

Burning for revenge after that avalanche of touchdowns, McKay got it in subsequent years. The Trojans won six, lost one and tied two of the last nine games he coached against the Irish. Later, the Fighting Irish went on a tear, winning 11 in a row from 1983 to 1993, during a 12–0–1 run (1983–1995), with a 17–17 tie in 1994.

The Trojans finally ended the drought in 1996. They were struggling at 5–6 and coming off a double-overtime loss to UCLA the previous week when the Irish came to town. Notre Dame took a 20–12 lead in the fourth quarter, but Jim Sanson's PAT try failed, leaving a ray of hope for the Trojans, eight points down. On the ensuing possession, USC drove 67 yards in eight plays, culminating in a 15-yard touchdown scamper by

Delon Washington, who also tied the game at 20 with a two-point conversion run. In overtime, Trojan quarterback Brad Otton hit Rodney Sermons with a five-yard touchdown pass to put his team up 27–20, and when Mark Cusano knocked down Ron Powlus's fourth-down pass attempt in ND's overtime possession, pandemonium erupted in the Coliseum with USC's first win in the series since 1982.

From 2002 through 2005, USC won two national titles, and Trojan players have captured three of the four Heisman Trophies, largely as a result of their play against the Irish. Quarterback Carson Palmer took home the hardware in 2002 after throwing for more yards (425) in one game against Notre Dame than anyone else ever had and leading the Trojans to another Notre Dame opponent record (since broken) of 610 total yards.

SC beat the Irish by 31 points that night. And again the next year. And the next, when quarterback Matt Leinart won the Heisman. The following season, 2005, Reggie Bush won the Heisman after running for 160 yards and touchdowns of 36, 45 and nine yards against the Irish. But the game had so much more than that. There were four lead changes in the fourth quarter alone. Late in the game the Irish led 31–28 with USC facing fourth-and-nine from its own 26. It was the Trojans' last chance to pull out a victory, and Leinart hit a streaking Dwayne Jarrett on a 61-yard pass play. With three seconds left, Leinart twisted into the end zone from a yard out for the 34–31 win.

Despite USC's recent domination, Notre Dame still leads the series 42 games to 30, with five ties.

——— USC-UCLA ———

Former UCLA coach Red Sanders once said that the UCLA–Southern California football series is not a matter of life and death. "It's more important than that," he said.

It is the unique collegiate rivalry. There are other traditional rivalries, but only USC-UCLA matches two major universities with renowned football programs located only 13 miles apart in a megalopolis.

Houston versus Rice fits the geographical requirements, but that's all.

When Southern California meets UCLA, families may be disrupted the week of the game. Father and mother, brothers and sisters may have gone to rival schools.

Among the many memorable games was a scoreless tie in 1939 before 103,000 at the Los Angeles Memorial Coliseum. Nor will the crowds through the years forget Gary Beban's late pass to beat Southern California 20–16 in 1965 in a game the Trojans had dominated, O.J. Simpson's climactic 64-yard touchdown

run in the 1967 game that Southern California won 21–20, or Erik Affholter's juggling catch in the end zone that defeated UCLA 17–13 in 1987.

The series, though, had a humble beginning.

UCLA was established in 1919 as the southern branch of the University of California, Berkeley, near downtown Los Angeles. The school outgrew its facilities and moved to its present campus in Westwood in 1929.

The University of Southern California was founded in 1880 and was playing football eight years later. By the late 1920s, the Trojans, gaining national identity with the inception of their series with Notre Dame, were a burgeoning power.

The crosstown rivalry, as such, began in 1929. Southern California won 76–0 to open the season and followed up with a 52–0 victory in 1930. Most often, though, the games have been dramatic, and with stirring endings.

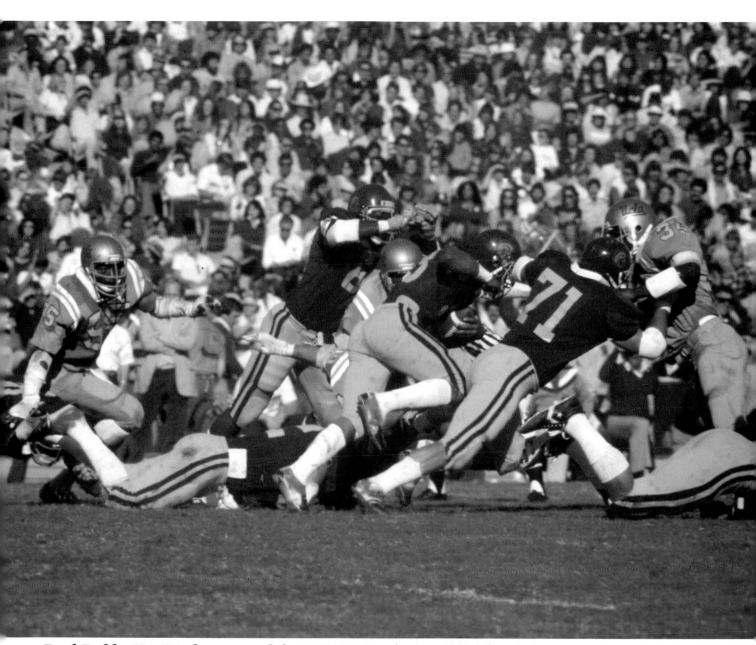

Brad Budde (No. 71) clears a path in USC's 17–10 win over UCLA in 1978.

USC quarterback John Fox displays an impaled Bruins head as his team's mascot looks on appreciatively after the Trojans' 17–7 win over UCLA in 1999.

In 1937, the Trojans were apparently on their way to a routine victory, leading 19–0 in the fourth quarter. Many in the crowd of 75,000 had already left when UCLA's Kenn Washington, a sophomore halfback, passed 62 yards in the air to halfback Hal Hirshon for a touchdown.

Hirshon had ranged far behind USC defenders because they didn't believe that Washington could possibly throw the ball that far. It was regarded at the time as one of the longest completed passes in college football history.

Washington, who became UCLA's first All-American in 1939, teamed with Hirshon again for a 44-yard touchdown pass less than a minute later. The surprising Bruins reached the Trojans' 15-yard line, but the USC defense dug in and held on for the 19–13 victory.

These were the days when the legendary Howard Jones coached the Trojan football team. The following year, Jones's 9–2 USC team rolled over the Bruins 42–7 on Thanksgiving Day, then finished out the regular season with a 13–0 shutout of Notre Dame and won the Rose Bowl 7–3 over Duke.

In 1939, a Rose Bowl berth was on the line for both teams. In the fourth quarter, UCLA drove 78 yards to a first down on the USC 3-yard line. Two running plays gained only two yards, and fullback Leo Cantor was thrown for a two-yard loss on third down.

What to do? A field-goal attempt seemed to be the percentage play, but, in democratic fashion, a vote was called for in the huddle by quarterback Ned Mathews. Five voted to go for a field goal, and five others opted to try for a touchdown. Mathews cast the deciding vote. He called a pass play.

It turned out to be the wrong decision, as Washington's pass intended for end Don MacPherson was knocked down by USC halfback Bobby Robertson.

So USC went to the Rose Bowl. The Trojans got the bid over the Bruins on the basis of fewer ties marring their conference record: 5–0–2 to 5–0–3.

USC and UCLA played each other eight times before the Bruins ever broke into the win column in the series. That was in 1942, when Bob Waterfield, who would later become a pro Hall of Fame quarterback with the Los Angeles Rams, threw the winning touchdown pass to end Burr Baldwin. The 14–7 win gave the Bruins their first outright Pacific Conference championship and sent them to the Rose Bowl for the first time.

The 1952 renewal was a matchup of unbeaten and untied teams for the first time in the series. The Trojans scored when wingback Al Carmichael, apparently stopped on a reverse, lateraled to halfback Jim Sears, who ran 75 yards for a touchdown. Later, USC guard Elmer Wilhoite intercepted a pass and returned it 72 yards to the UCLA 8-yard line. From there, Sears passed to Carmichael for a touchdown and the 14–12 win.

The 1967 meeting was the showcase game of the series. Everything was on the line: the Rose Bowl bid, a possible (actually, eventual) national championship and the Heisman Trophy.

Beban, a senior now, and Simpson, the electrifying junior tailback, were the primary Heisman candidates at the time.

UCLA coach Tommy Prothro had come up with a novel defensive plan against Simpson. After every carry, Prothro's players were to help Simpson to his feet immediately so he wouldn't have the opportunity to rest.

"At first it bugged me when those UCLA cats picked me up," O.J. recalled years later, after having joined the Buffalo Bills and, in 1973, having become the first pro to top the 2,000-yard barrier in single-season rushing.

"But as the game wore on and I started getting tired, I sort of looked forward to them picking me up. In fact, one of their guys was slow on a particular play, and I chided him, saying, 'Come on, man, I'm waiting.'"

The game lived up to every aspect of its advance billing. Beban, playing courageously with a painful rib injury, enhanced his

Reggie Bush leaps into history, clinching the Heisman with this touchdown run against UCLA in 2005, in a game the Trojans won handily, 66–19.

Heisman prospects by passing for 301 yards and two touchdowns.

As a result, the Bruins led 20–14 in the fourth quarter, and Simpson said that the momentum of the game had apparently shifted in UCLA's favor. And so it seemed when the Trojans were confronted with a third-and-eight situation at their own 36-yard line.

Simpson recalled, "Our quarterback, Toby Page, originally called a pass play; then he yelled, 'Red alert,' meaning the next number would be an audible."

The play was a USC staple, 23 Blast, calling for Simpson to run between tackle and guard on the left side. Simpson was thinking first down, but he got more than that, cutting back to the middle of the field and, with his sprinter's speed, outrunning the Bruins to the end zone.

Although USC coach John McKay was accustomed to brilliant runs by Simpson, he nevertheless said: "A good back might have made eight yards for a first down. O.J. made it to the Rose Bowl. It was the damnedest run I've ever seen. The very first time I saw him run the ball in spring practice [in 1967], I knew I had a very special player."

Beban, though, won the Heisman Trophy in 1967. Simpson would claim it in 1968.

Not all the activity has been on the field in this series. With the schools located within relatively short driving distance, campus raids have been commonplace. UCLA students have been known to splash blue paint on the statue of Tommy Trojan on the Southern California campus.

In 1958, USC journalism students distributed a bogus *Daily Bruin* newspaper, replete with Trojan propaganda, on the UCLA campus. Copies of the real *Daily Bruin* were confiscated. Unsuspecting UCLA students were shocked to read demeaning stories about their team and coaches. That year some UCLA students tried to sully the Tommy Trojan statue with fertilizer dropped from a helicopter but missed the target. USC maintenance

crews now cover the statue with plastic and canvas during the week of the USC-UCLA game.

Another time a USC student masquerading as a UCLA student became a member of the UCLA rally committee in charge of card stunts. The Trojan infiltrator altered the instruction sheet, and on game day, every UCLA card stunt was marred by a small, block USC in the corner of the section.

And, of course, the game has a trophy, the Victory Bell, which was originally owned by UCLA in 1939. Then, after a truce, it became the symbol of victory, with the winner taking temporary possession.

UCLA owned the Victory Bell for eight straight years, winning every matchup from 1991 to 1998. But beginning in 1999, the Trojans took back control of the series. In 2001, Pete Carroll's first year at the USC helm, the Men of Troy held the Bruins to 114 total yards and 10 first downs, snagging three interceptions in the process. Antuan

Simmons returned one of the picks 36 yards for a touchdown, quarterback Carson Palmer connected with tight end Kori Dickerson on a 66-yard catch-and-run for another score, and tailback Chris Howard scampered 34 yards for another touchdown in USC's 27–0 shutout win that day. The Trojans won back-to-back national championships in 2003 and 2004, with wins of 47–22 and 29–24, respectively, over UCLA. In the closer-than-expected 2004 contest, USC tailback Reggie Bush scored on runs of 65 and 81 yards among his 335 total-yard output that day.

Bush then made the 2005 matchup his personal Heisman showcase, rushing for 260 yards and two touchdowns in USC's 66–19 laugher. LenDale White added 154 yards of his own as the Trojans amassed an astounding 697 yards of total offense, including 448 on the ground.

USC has now won seven in a row in the series and leads 41 games to 27, with seven ties.

Reggie Bush

TALKIN' USC FOOTBALL

We thought we'd go straight to the source and let some of Southern California's greatest legends share their thoughts about Trojan football along with other observers who know what they're talking about.

"*I had no doubt.* *We never gave up and kept fighting. That's why we're the No. 1 team in the country."* —REGGIE BUSH, AFTER USC'S 34–31 WIN OVER NOTRE DAME IN SOUTH BEND

"I'm enjoying this too much. *Why should I leave?"* —MATT LEINART, ANNOUNCING HIS DECISION TO STAY AT USC FOR HIS SENIOR SEASON

"I think they're great, *but I don't know if that's a surprise to anybody. We felt that way a week ago, and they proved it today. I think they're an excellent team. They play great as a team. You look at them today. They have no turnovers, just really executed in a great way, and they made the plays that counted. ... They made the plays where it really mattered."* —OKLAHOMA COACH BOB STOOPS ON THE DOMINANCE OF THE 2004 TROJANS

"It wasn't easy, but we made it look that way. *I think this was as close to perfect as you can get in this kind of setting, high pressure."* —USC TIGHT END DOMINIQUE BYRD, WHOSE 33-YARD TOUCHDOWN RECEPTION WAS THE TROJANS' FIRST SCORE IN THE 55–19 ORANGE BOWL ROUT OF OKLAHOMA THAT GAVE USC THE 2004 NATIONAL CHAMPIONSHIP

Matt Leinart

John Robinson

"Thank you, John Robinson. *I know you are here. You taught me how to compete at USC. You gave me so much."* —RONNIE LOTT, IN HIS NFL HALL OF FAME INDUCTION SPEECH

"One of the most impressive things *he did was turn around the series with Notre Dame. He lost only one of his last nine games against the Irish (going 6-1-2)—and eight of those were against the great Ara Parseghian. He was demanding, decisive and outspoken, but he was also charming, loyal and, at times, even shy. And he was one of the funniest public speakers in America."* —USC QUARTERBACK PAT HADEN ON JOHN MCKAY

"Somehow, I always feel better *with Charles White standing next to me. He was the toughest, most intense running back I've ever coached."* —JOHN ROBINSON

"What I did doesn't mean all that much right now. All I'm thinking about is that we didn't win."* —A TEAM-ORIENTED MARCUS ALLEN, AFTER USC LOST 13–3 TO WASHINGTON STATE IN A GAME IN WHICH ALLEN SURPASSED THE 2,000-YARD BARRIER FOR THE SEASON, BECOMING THE FIRST PLAYER IN NCAA HISTORY TO DO SO*

"People call me the greatest player in that rivalry.

That's the greatest thing anyone could say about me. The thing that amazes me, I don't know if anyone gets talked to about the same game every year for 30 years. You got to carry on the legacy of that game and know the legacy of the game itself. It's not that team you're beating; it's the legacy of the team. I'm honored to be able to play in the game." —ANTHONY DAVIS ON THE USC–NOTRE DAME RIVALRY. DAVIS SCORED 11 TOUCHDOWNS IN THREE GAMES AGAINST THE IRISH.

"It's not going to be an instant classic. But it's a game that will go down in history."* —REGGIE BUSH ON THE 2005 ORANGE BOWL*

Marcus Allen

─── The Quotable John McKay ───

In addition to winning four national championships during his tenure at USC, John McKay was one of the most quotable figures in sports history. Here's a small sample of his wit and wisdom.

"The more I win, the more I can't stand the thought of losing."

On recruiting his son, John: *"I had a rather distinct advantage. I slept with his mother."*

On losing: *"Boy, do I hate to see that scene in the dressing room where a player gets up with tears in his eyes and says, 'We'll get 'em next year.' 'Damn it,' I think, 'why didn't we get them this year? Don't worry about the next one. Next year may come and we may all be dead.'"*

McKay's halftime speech to his team, *trailing Notre Dame 17–0 in 1964 (USC came back to win 20–17): "If you don't score more than 17 points, you'll lose."*

"Intensity is a lot of guys who run fast."

"Does a team have to be emotional to win? *Well, I've always said nobody is more emotional than Corky [McKay's wife], and she can't play football worth a damn."*

"I'll never be hung in effigy. *Before every season, I send my men out to buy up all the rope in Los Angeles."*

"We don't beat people *with surprises but with execution."*

"God's busy. *They have to make do with me."* —ON WHETHER HIS TEAM PRAYED FOR VICTORY

"I'm in favor of it." —MCKAY, THEN THE HEAD COACH OF THE TAMPA BAY BUCS, WHEN ASKED ABOUT HIS TEAM'S EXECUTION

"He gets faster in the fourth quarter, *and I get smarter."* —ON HIS HABIT OF LETTING O.J. SIMPSON TAKE OVER AS THE GAME WORE ON

John McKay accepts the 1962 Associated Press national championship trophy.

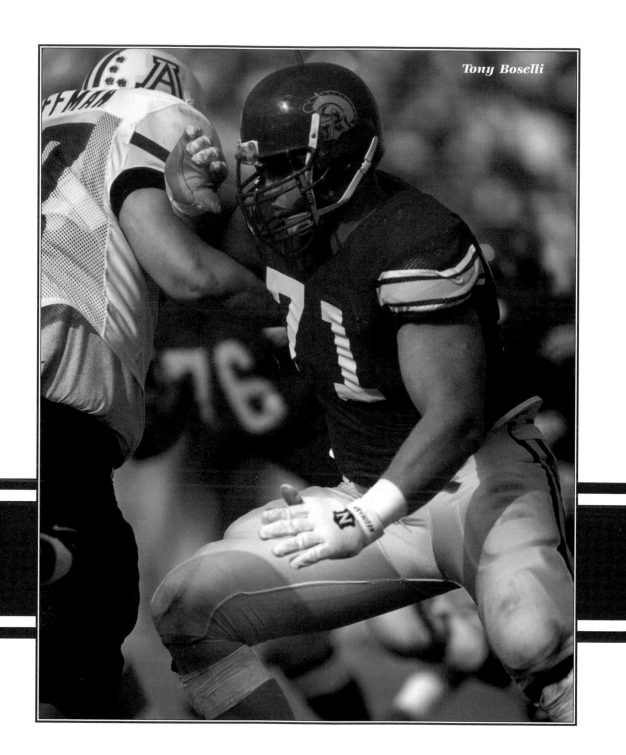

Tony Boselli

FACTS AND FIGURES

—— Bowl Tradition ——

USC has been one of college football's greatest postseason performers. In 44 postseason appearances, the Trojans have emerged victorious from 28 of them.

RECORD: 28-16

1923 Rose Bowl	USC 14, Penn State 3
1924 Christmas Festival	USC 20, Missouri 7
1930 Rose Bowl	USC 47, Pittsburgh 14
1932 Rose Bowl	USC 21, Tulane 12
1933 Rose Bowl	USC 35, Pittsburgh 0
1939 Rose Bowl	USC 7, Duke 3
1940 Rose Bowl	USC 14, Tennessee 0
1944 Rose Bowl	USC 29, Washington 0
1945 Rose Bowl	USC 25, Tennessee 0
1946 Rose Bowl	Alabama 34, USC 14
1948 Rose Bowl	Michigan 49, USC 0

(continued on next page)

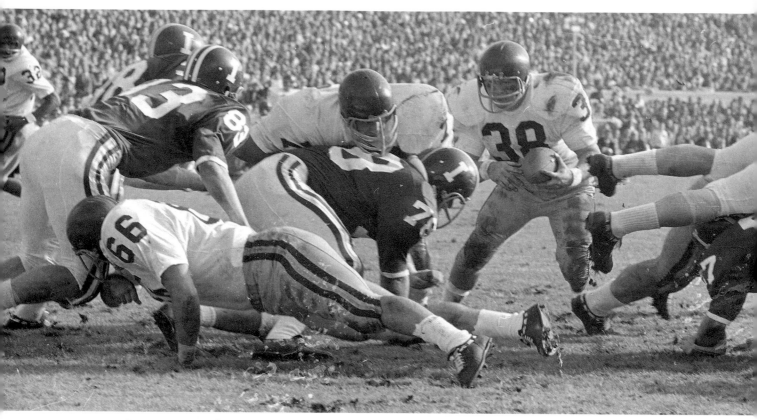

1968 Rose Bowl

(continued)	
1953 Rose Bowl	USC 7, Wisconsin 0
1955 Rose Bowl	Ohio State 20, USC 7
1963 Rose Bowl	USC 42, Wisconsin 37
1967 Rose Bowl	Purdue 14, USC 13
1968 Rose Bowl	USC 14, Indiana 3
1969 Rose Bowl	Ohio State 27, USC 16
1970 Rose Bowl	USC 10, Michigan 3
1973 Rose Bowl	USC 42, Ohio State 17

1974 Rose Bowl	Ohio State 42, USC 21
1975 Rose Bowl	USC 18, Ohio State 17
1975 Liberty Bowl	USC 20, Texas A&M 0
1977 Rose Bowl	USC 14, Michigan 6
1977 Blucbonnet Bowl	USC 47, Texas A&M 28
1979 Rose Bowl	USC 17, Michigan 10
1980 Rose Bowl	USC 17, Ohio State 16
1982 Fiesta Bowl	Penn State 26, USC 10
1985 Rose Bowl	USC 20, Ohio State 17
1985 Aloha Bowl	Alabama 24, USC 3
1987 Florida Citrus Bowl	Auburn 16, USC 7
1988 Rose Bowl	Michigan State 20, USC 17
1989 Rose Bowl	Michigan 22, USC 14
1990 Rose Bowl	USC 17, Michigan 10
1990 John Hancock Bowl	Michigan State 17, USC 16
1992 Freedom Bowl	Fresno State 24, USC 7
1993 Freedom Bowl	USC 28, Utah 21
1995 Cotton Bowl	USC 55, Texas Tech 14
1996 Rose Bowl	USC 41, Northwestern 32
1998 Sun Bowl	TCU 28, USC 19
2001 Las Vegas Bowl	Utah 10, USC 6
2003 Orange Bowl	USC 38, Iowa 17
2004 Rose Bowl	USC 28, Michigan 14
2005 Orange Bowl	USC 55, Oklahoma 19
2006 Rose Bowl	Texas 41, USC 38

— USC in the —
College Football Hall of Fame

NAME	POSITION	YEARS	INDUCTED
Marcus Allen	Halfback	1978–1981	2000
Jon Arnett	Halfback	1954–1956	2001
John Baker	Guard	1929–1931	1983
Ricky Bell	Running Back	1973–1976	2003
Tay Brown	Tackle	1930–1932	1980

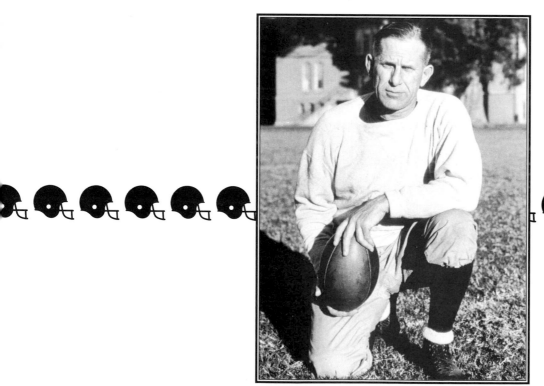

Howard Jones

John McKay

NAME	POSITION	YEARS	INDUCTED
Brad Budde	Guard	1976–1979	1998
Paul Cleary	End	1946–1947	1989
Anthony Davis	Running Back	1972–1974	2005
Morley Drury	Quarterback	1925–1927	1954
John Ferraro	Tackle	1943–1944,	
		1946–1947	1974
Mike Garrett	Halfback	1963–1965	1985
Frank Gifford	Halfback	1949–1951	1975
Howard Jones	Coach	1925–1940	1951
Mort Kaer	Halfback	1924–1926	1972
Ronnie Lott	Safety	1977–1980	2002
John McKay	Coach	1960–1975	1988

(continued on next page)

(continued)

NAME	POSITION	YEARS	INDUCTED
Mike McKeever	Guard	1958–1960	1987
Dan McMillan	Tackle	1917, 1919–1921	1971
Erny Pinckert	Halfback	1929–1931	1957
Marvin Powell	Tackle	1974–1976	1994
Aaron Rosenberg	Guard	1931–1933	1966
O.J. Simpson	Halfback	1967–1968	1983
Ernie Smith	Tackle	1930–1932	1970
Harry Smith	Guard	1937–1939	1955
Lynn Swann	Wide Receiver	1971–1973	1993
Cotton Warburton	Quarterback	1932–1934	1975
Charles White	Halfback	1976–1979	1996
Ron Yary	Tackle	1965–1967	1987
Charles Young	Tight End	1970–1972	2004

Carson Palmer

Career Statistical Leaders

Rushes: 1,147, Charles White

Rushing Yards: 6,245, Charles White

Pass Attempts: 1,569, Carson Palmer

Pass Completions: 927, Carson Palmer

Passing Yards: 11,818, Carson Palmer

(continued on next page)

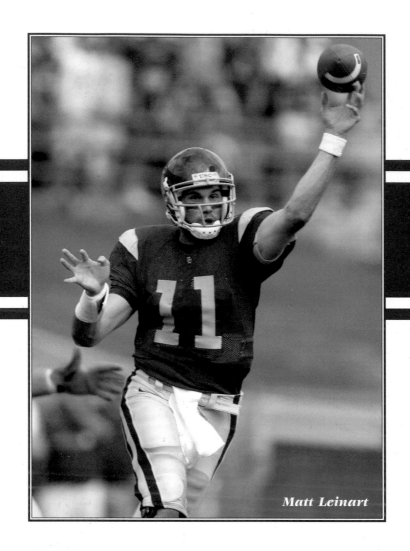

Matt Leinart

(continued)

Passing Touchdowns: 99, Matt Leinart

Receptions: 207, Keary Colbert

Receiving Yards: 3,201, Johnnie Morton

Touchdown Receptions: 30, Mike Williams

Interceptions: 20, Artimus Parker

Mike Williams